ADVANCE PRAISE

"David is a digital marketing pioneer and highly successful entrepreneur whom I have had the privilege of getting to know personally. His subject matter expertise and real-life experience as a successful founder make Unfair Marketing an extremely valuable resource for any business leader."

—PENNY PRITZKER, CHAIRMAN AND FOUNDER, PSP PARTNERS; FORMER US SECRETARY OF COMMERCE

"David Rodnitzky is a genius. Not because he's more complex than the rest of us (although he probably is), but because he thinks more clearly and simply about marketing than the rest of us! His book just makes perfect sense. Nothing is more useful than that."

—BOB GUCCIONE JR., FOUNDER, WONDERLUST, SPIN, AND GEAR

"David Rodnitzky is a recognized leader in digital marketing. Through his work with the world's most innovative and

demanding companies, he has pioneered many of the ROI-boosting best practices that savvy marketers worldwide use for their own campaigns."

—FREDERICK VALLAEYS, CEO, OPTMYZR;
FORMER GOOGLE ADWORDS EVANGELIST

"I've worked with David Rodnitzky for more than 15 years. He is an amazing digital marketer who is highly respected for his ability to deliver outstanding performance across all marketing channels."

—SAAR GUR, PARTNER, CHARLES RIVER VENTURES

"In the wild and ever-changing world of digital marketing, it's difficult for marketing leaders to constantly keep pace with new techniques and strategies. The expectations for ROI are constant, and savvy marketers need a digital marketing partner that they can trust. David knows his stuff and provides practical and relevant advice to keep marketers on the top of their game."

—TAMI BHAUMIK, VICE PRESIDENT
OF MARKETING, ROBLOX

"David was the first person I met in the digital marketing industry, and seeing his passion for work is what got me excited to also build a career in marketing. When I met him, he was one of the earliest SEM experts in the world, and over the years, I've seen him conquer marketing on every channel better than others. I consider him a friend and mentor, and his notes on *digital marketing should be as insightful as you could ever read."*

—ADAM FOROUGHI, CEO AND FOUNDER, APPLOVIN

"Full of best practices based on actual client experience, this book can immediately help your business grow. David Rodnitzky and 3Q are synonymous with cutting-edge digital marketing and delivering performance. This is the one book on digital marketing you have to read for 2021."

—CHRIS LIEN, CEO, MARIN SOFTWARE

"Every entrepreneur will benefit from reading David Rodnitzky's book on digital marketing—a powerful framework for growing your business with strategies straight from 3Q Digital, one of the most well-respected agencies in Silicon Valley."

—DAVID BAGA, CEO, EVEN

"David Rodnitzky is my go-to guy in Silicon Valley for digital marketing. He always seems to be a few years ahead of the competition and, as a result, is able to consistently produce superior marketing outcomes."

—DAVID YUAN, GENERAL PARTNER,
TECHNOLOGY CROSSOVER VENTURES

"I've been in online marketing for most of my career, and I've always had tremendous respect for David Rodnitzky and 3Q Digital. I wish this book had been around a few years sooner—it would have saved me a lot of time and a ton of money!"

—LARRY KIM, CEO, MOBILEMONKEY

"3Q Digital is the most well-respected digital agency in Silicon Valley, if not the United States. 3Q has worked with the world's most innovative and demanding companies and consistently delivers massive ROI to their clients."

—MEAGEN EISENBERG, CMO, TRIPACTIONS

"If you read one book on digital marketing this year, read this one. David Rodnitzky and his crew at 3Q are synonymous with cutting-edge digital marketing. This book is full of best practices and insider secrets that will immediately improve your marketing game."

—RON SCHNEIDERMAN, CEO, ALLTRAILS

"David and 3Q have always been leaders in digital and growth marketing. In Unfair Marketing, David shares some of the best practices he and his team have honed over the years and implemented for well-known clients. Every digital marketer could learn from his experience."

—ROBERT GLAZER, CEO, ACCELERATION PARTNERS

UNFAIR MARKETING

UNFAIR MARKETING

Drive Marketing Success by Leveraging Your Company's Unique Strengths

DAVID RODNITZKY

MODERN MARKETING **MASTERS**

UNFAIR MARKETING
*Drive Marketing Success by Leveraging Your
Company's Unique Strengths*

ISBN   978-1-5445-0664-7 *Hardcover*
        978-1-5445-0662-3 *Paperback*
        978-1-5445-0663-0 *Ebook*

To Rebecca, Zev, and Sammy—my ultimate unfair advantages!

CONTENTS

INTRODUCTION

My 10-year-old son is convinced that the world is plotting against him. Every day he comes home from school with a tale of injustice.

"Daddy, today the girls in class were making fun of the boys, and when we tried to tell them to stop, *we* got in trouble."

"The fourth-grade math class got cupcakes yesterday and didn't share them, but today when we got cupcakes, the teacher made us share them with the fourth graders!"

He's learning an important lesson: the world isn't fair. Bad things happen to good people. People cheat and get away with it. And yes, sometimes cupcakes are only shared in one direction.

When confronted with unfairness, we have a choice. We can loudly protest and hope that the world comes to its senses; we can sit idly, pout, and do nothing; or we can fight back.

To be clear, the right response varies based on the situation. Given that this is a business book, we're not going to get all philosophical and talk about the times in history when civil disobedience or violent resistance was the only choice. This is not a discourse on Thomas Paine's *Common Sense* or Martin Luther King Jr's *Letter from a Birmingham Jail*.

From a business perspective, I got a great piece of advice early in my career: "You don't get what you deserve; you get what you negotiate." Put another way, business is unfair, so the only way to win in business is to find your own unfair advantage.

And that's what this book is about: unfair marketing advantages.

This book is not about doing anything illegal or unethical. You can create an unfair marketing advantage without breaking any laws or even feeling dirty. What I mean by unfair in this context is simple: *discover something inside your company that gives you an advantage that the competition simply can't copy.*

Imagine, for example, that you go to a high school, and it

just so happens that a kid in your town is over seven feet tall and can jump twice as high as the average person. Is it unethical for your high school basketball team to use this giant to win a lot of games? Of course not! Is it unfair? Well, yes, in the sense that the rival teams that don't have a super-athletic seven-footer don't really stand a chance. That's what I mean by an unfair advantage.

The challenge for a lot of businesses is that finding their unfair marketing advantage is not as easy as the high school basketball coach who sees the future NBA star walk into the gym. Many companies have powerful unfair marketing advantages that they are either underutilizing or not using at all. So this book has two objectives: first, to identify common unfair marketing advantages that I've observed over my 20 years in marketing, and second, to give you examples that show you how other companies have driven massive marketing success by using these techniques.

MY PERSONAL UNFAIR ADVANTAGE STORY

I live in the San Francisco Bay Area, where our pro football team is the 49ers, named after the pioneers who flooded California after the 1849 discovery of gold in the foothills of the Sierra Nevada mountains. I frequently take my family to the area of the gold discovery (known, not surprisingly, as Gold Country). We've visited a few mine sites and museums dedicated to the gold rush.

In the very early days of the gold rush, it was relatively easy to find gold. There were literally nuggets lying on the ground that prospectors could just pick up. Once these "easy pickings" were all scooped up, prospectors had to pan for gold, then dig for gold, and then eventually build mines with hazardous chemicals, high-pressure water cannons, and miles of dangerous tunnels and heavy machinery.

Most miners didn't get rich, and sadly, many died at a young age, either because of illness (often caused by exposure to hazardous chemicals) or mining accidents.

I came to the Bay Area in 1999, 150 years after the 49ers arrived in California. It so happens that I arrived in San Francisco in the middle of another gold rush: this time, the dot-com boom. I actually didn't come to San Francisco for the dot-com boom. I mainly came because I just wanted to be near the ocean after living my entire life in the Midwest, but I quickly got caught up in the gold rush. I landed a job at a trendy dot-com that had just received $20 million from two prominent venture capital firms, and I received a grant of 10,000 stock options in the company. I assumed that my stock would be worth at least $1 million, and I felt that I was living the American dream.

Alas, like the gold prospectors of 1849, the boom became a bust very quickly. My startup struggled to convince businesses to use our software (we were too far ahead of our time, among other issues). Our venture capital money dwindled, and then the entire dot-com ecosystem collapsed. Hundreds of startups closed shop, and many of my fellow internet pioneers suddenly found themselves out of a job with a very expensive monthly rent payment hanging over their head.

Over the course of a couple of years, hundreds of thousands of people left the dot-com world behind and moved out of the Bay Area, deciding to pursue more stable jobs in lower-cost towns. And while San Francisco didn't become a ghost town like many of the mining towns in Gold Country that disappeared overnight after the Gold Rush ended, the decrease in population and enthusiasm was noticeable.

The gold rushes of 1849 and 1999 were both based on the same myth: if you work hard, are willing to take risks, and get in early on a trend, you will become incredibly rich. In reality, this almost never happens. Yes, there were a few people who picked up gold nuggets off the ground and made a ton of money, and there were some early dot-com founders who launched businesses and got them acquired for millions of dollars with minimal effort. These folks are actually about as lucky as the winner of a $500 million lotto ticket.

The folks who really got wealthy in the gold rush and the dot-com boom did so because they created unfair advantages for themselves. In the case of the gold rush, it was the businessmen who set up large-scale mines or innovative supply chains who became rich. Wikipedia notes, "The wealthiest man in California during the early years of the rush was Samuel Brannan, a tireless self-promoter, shopkeeper and newspaper publisher. Brannan opened the first supply stores in Sacramento, Coloma, and other spots in the goldfields. Just as the rush began he purchased all the prospecting supplies available in San Francisco and re-sold them at a substantial profit."[1] Note all the unfair advantages inherent in this paragraph: unfair publicity (he owned newspapers!), first-mover advantage, and a monopoly on supplies.

In 1999, most pundits believed that the battle for search engine dominance was over. The clear winners in search were Lycos, Yahoo, Excite, AltaVista, and Infoseek. All of these sites were making tons of money and saw little incentive to change their profitable ways. But a couple of PhDs from Stanford built an algorithm that was fundamentally better than all of the leading players, and with an incredible data advantage, they were able to deliver better results, faster, and without the pervasive advertisements that smothered the organic results on the other search engines. By the time the competitors realized how obsolete their search engines were, Google had built an unfair brand

---

1   "California Gold Rush," Wikipedia, last modified April 6, 2021, https://en.wikipedia.org/wiki/California_Gold_Rush#Profits.

advantage and backed it up with superior technology, such that people would just "Google it" rather than "search it."

Luck and first-mover advantage are always helpful, but massively successful businesses don't actually need either. Instead, successful businesses find ways to gain an unfair advantage over the competition.

In 2008, after nine years of working as an employee at other people's startups, I started my digital marketing agency (then PPCAdBuying, later PPC Associates, but today known as 3Q Digital). I wasn't the first digital agency by more than a decade; the timing wasn't particularly great (it was the beginning of the Great Recession), and I had no proprietary technology. I did, however, have two unfair advantages.

First, I had been practicing search engine marketing (SEM) since almost the day it was invented, which meant that I had a lot more knowledge about how to make it profitable than most other people. And second, I had spent a decade in Silicon Valley building genuine relationships with successful entrepreneurs and investors.

As such, when I announced I was starting a digital agency, the combination of superior knowledge and a great network led to a continuous flow of referrals to potential clients. And now—13 years in—3Q Digital is an established brand—

another unfair advantage—so we win a lot of business simply because of our brand's reputation for thoughtful, data-driven, ROI-producing marketing.

To be clear, I didn't just accept these unfair advantages; I exploited them. Using my long history of SEM expertise, I found ways to get free publicity—via guest blog posts, becoming a columnist in industry publications, and getting regular speaking opportunities at leading conferences. Search my name on Google, and you will see the hundreds of articles, interviews, and presentations that I've given over the years. My unfair knowledge advantage became an unfair publicity advantage and eventually created an unfair brand advantage.

Similarly, as I made connections with investors and founders, I often asked these connections to introduce me to similar business influencers. After a few years, I started to hear the same story from every inbound lead: "I asked person A who we should use for digital marketing, and they said 3Q Digital. Then I asked person B, and they said the same. Then I went onto a message board for founders, and everyone recommended 3Q Digital." In many instances, I would get intros from people who I had never met and who had never worked with 3Q—they had just heard about 3Q from so many influential people in Silicon Valley that they assumed we were the best agency.

Around the time I was starting my agency, the California Lotto was running ads on TV with the slogan "Somebody's gonna [win the] lotto. Might as well be you." Earlier I noted that relying on luck and a first-mover advantage to achieve business success was akin to buying a lotto ticket and expecting to become a millionaire. From that perspective, I think that this lotto slogan is ridiculous—yes, someone will win the lotto, but it is almost certain that it will not be you!

That said, what I do like about this slogan is this: **in whatever business you start or profession you enter, someone is going to be number one. Someone is going to create the number one digital agency. Someone is going to be recognized as the best marketer. Someone is going to become the CMO of the company you are currently at. And the question I asked myself back in 2008 was this: why not you?** Why should someone else be number one? What can you do to get to the top?

Again, this is not about luck—this is the opposite of luck. What can you do to maximize your chance of success? The gold miners who arrived early, picked up a few nuggets, and just stayed content to keep finding a few nuggets the way they always had were surpassed by entrepreneurs who found better, more efficient and scalable ways to find gold. So, too, was the fate of early search engines that didn't bother to innovate like Google.

The winners in every field of business have two things in common: they work hard, and they exploit their unfair advantages. This doesn't mean cheating, being a jerk, or waging war against the competition. Rather, they constantly look for advantages that their business has and maximize them. It is really that simple, yet most businesses don't identify or act on their unfair advantages.

HOW TO CREATE YOUR OWN UNFAIR ADVANTAGE

This is a book about marketing. I'll discuss more than 50 ways to create unfair marketing advantages for your business. If you can leverage half of these ideas, you will see measurable business improvement. But don't stop there. Find unfair advantages in your finance department, HR, sales, product, and so on. After all, if you don't, your competition will. Somebody's gonna win the lotto, and somebody's gonna leverage their unfair advantages—it might as well be you!

The book is divided into five chapters that will each cover an unfair advantage:

Chapter 1 covers unfair **data** advantages. I'll discuss the types of data that you have inside your company, how you can access this data, and then how you can use it to outflank your competition.

Chapter 2 is about unfair **knowledge** advantages. This chapter discusses the importance of experts who have micro-specialized knowledge and how you can use these people to save you time and money over competitors who reinvent the wheel by relying on generalists.

Chapter 3 is about unfair **access** advantages. Here I'll discuss how you can uncover special relationships that allow you to get free PR and identify advertising opportunities that are available to you and not competitors.

Chapter 4 is about unfair **brand** advantages. This chapter shows you how to leverage your existing brand recognition to create unequal playing fields beyond your standard branding efforts. This includes using your brand to actually save money on your direct response marketing and generating free visibility because other companies want to leverage your brand in their marketing.

Chapter 5 is about unfair **money** advantages. This chapter focuses on three types of companies: companies that have a lot of funding and can literally outspend the competition, companies that make more money on a transaction than their peers, and companies that can make products cheaper than others. Each of these leads to massive unfair marketing advantages.

WHO SHOULD READ THIS BOOK?

This book has been structured to provide value for both the novice marketer and the world-class expert. Each chapter starts with basic definitions of key terms and explanations of concepts so that a beginning marketer can understand the opportunity to benefit from a specific unfair advantage. In some cases, simply knowing that an unfair advantage exists is enough to give your business a huge boost. In others, technical expertise is necessary to execute the unfair advantage (meaning, I don't recommend you try to use the technique without the assistance of an expert). I'll call out which techniques require help and which do not.

Once I've covered the basics, I'll move into more advanced strategies that are designed to bolster the existing knowledge of more seasoned marketers. This will include a discussion about the sophisticated technology and math that are often necessary to compete at the highest levels. For the novice marketer, much of this discussion will seem like a foreign language. For the expert, I hope that I'll provide at least a few ideas in every chapter that you haven't thought of that will move your marketing forward.

I also strongly believe that non-marketers—in particular, business owners—will benefit from this book. The core concept in this book—the idea that every business has something unique about it that can give it an unfair advantage—is a new way of thinking about your business. Once you understand the concept of unfair marketing, you will look at your business differently and start to see things in your business that you previously ignored as powerful benefits.

Your company is great and special. If it weren't, you'd be working somewhere else. The goal of this book is to help you identify the unique and amazing things about your company that you can use to turbocharge your marketing. Let's work together to make sure you get more cupcakes than you have to give (note: I believe in equal sharing of cupcakes among kids; this is a metaphor only). Welcome to unfair marketing!

CHAPTER 1

YOUR UNFAIR DATA ADVANTAGE

In the 1980s comedy *Back to the Future Part II*, Biff—the villain of the movie—travels back in time to the 1950s and takes with him an almanac with the scores of every sports game ever. Evil person that he is, he uses the almanac to place bets on sports, knowing that every bet is 100 percent certain to pay off! He becomes incredibly wealthy and uses his wealth to become very powerful and, of course, even more evil.

This is a common theme in movies: the omniscient—or all-knowing—villain. Someone who has information that others don't and uses it for evil.

Imagine what it would be like to be an omniscient marketer.

You would know that every dollar you spent on an advertising campaign was certain to produce 10X return, that your branding was going to stick in the minds of your target customer, and that your PR efforts would drive massive viral attention for your company. Your market domination would be inevitable!

Alas, barring the invention of a time machine, there's never a 100 percent guarantee that your marketing will hit the mark, but you and Biff from *Back to the Future* do have one thing in common: you have access to data that others do not, and you can use this secret data to drive profit and market share. This is the first unfair marketing advantage: a data advantage.

We all have access to a lot of data. You should ensure that you have a way to track this data. There is internal business data about customers, competitors, products, finances, employees, and locations and external data points about the economy, the weather, politics, historical trends, and so on. Indeed, we have so much data that it often causes more confusion than it provides good answers. (I often describe this problem by paraphrasing a hip-hop song: "Mo' data, mo' problems.")

Every company—no matter how small—has data that can create a business advantage. Even if you just sell one $10 product a day, you have data that your competitors don't (what product is it? Who bought it? Where do they live? etc.). While big companies usually have more data than small companies, all companies have actionable, proprietary data!

Thus, this overwhelming trove of data is both a threat and an opportunity. Companies that figure out how to extract learnings from their data will make smarter marketing decisions than the competition, whereas companies that can't understand how to use their data will be outflanked and lose market share.

Let me give you a simple example of how data can be the difference between marketing success and failure. Let's say that there are two companies buying TV advertising. They each sell the exact same product, a blue widget. They also have the exact same advertising budget.

Both companies start their TV campaigns by spending $1,000 on two different TV shows. The only difference between these two companies is that Company A changes their toll-free number based on the TV show, and Company B uses the same toll-free number for each show. So, for example, when Company A advertises their widgets on *The Late Show with Stephen Colbert*, they use the toll-free number 1-800-555-1212, and then when they run an ad on *CNN Tonight*, they use a different toll-free number—1-800-555-1213. As a result, when someone places an order, they instantly know which TV show drove that order because the person is calling via a unique phone number.

At the end of the week, each advertiser has seen their $1,000 budget result in only $800 in sales. Company B is dejected and concludes that TV advertising must not work for their business, so they stop advertising. Company A, however, looks at the data they have collected and comes to a different conclusion. They see that they spent $500 on *CNN Tonight* and drove $700 of sales, but the $500 they spent on *The Late Show with Stephen Colbert* only drove $100 of sales. So instead of shutting down their TV campaign, they shift all of their budget to CNN. The next week, they spend $1,000 and get $1,400 of sales!

Company A created an unfair data advantage. By coming up with a way to measure performance at a granular level, they were able to cut advertising that was unprofitable and increase spend on profitable ads. Meanwhile, Company B's marketing team is scratching their heads, trying to figure out why Company A keeps advertising on TV when it seems so unprofitable!

Note that Company A didn't have access to information that Company B couldn't also access—the difference here is that Company A came up with a way to measure the data that Company B did not. And that made all the difference and drove profit and ultimately business growth!

If you've skimmed through the book, you've noticed that this first chapter is substantially larger than all those that follow it. There are two reasons for this difference: first, creating a data advantage is almost always the most important (and unfair!) advantage you can build for your business. And second, getting a handle on your data is complicated. It requires a lot of foundational knowledge in statistics, programming, marketing, strategy, and analysis.

So this is broken into multiple parts, with each section creating a foundation upon which the subsequent sections will build. The first section will help you understand the types of proprietary data you might have. Next, you'll learn how to track and collect this proprietary data.

The third section describes how to normalize your data, allowing you to make apples-to-apples comparisons. Last but not least, section four teaches you how to make all of this data actionable so that you can make business decisions that drive profit and market share growth.

As you embark on your journey to create an unfair data advantage, it may feel like an overwhelming task with no end. If you have perfectionist tendencies like me, you'll want to quit many times along the way as you find inconsistencies in your data or you realize that you don't have all the tools you need to make the best conclusions. In these moments, think about two adages: "don't let the perfect get in the way of the good" and "a journey of a thousand miles begins with a single step." You might see these phrases come up throughout this book, for good reason: creating unfair advantages is challenging—if it wasn't, everyone would be doing it, and the advantage would be nullified.

WHERE IS MY DATA?

In a moment, I'll discuss the four types of unfair data advantages you can create (the previous example showcases one of these: better measurement). First, however, it's worth discussing where you can find your data. In the previous example, Company A used toll-free numbers to collect data on which TV show was driving sales. You could organize this data by having someone in your call center write down every sale from each toll-free number and then give you the notebook with all of the data, but savvy marketers have moved beyond note-taking to aggregating their data.

Today, modern marketers use a suite of technologies to capture data and allow for analysis of millions or billions of different data points (you'd need a big notebook to capture this much info!). The most common tools in use include the following.

CUSTOMER RELATIONSHIP MANAGEMENT (CRM) SOFTWARE

A CRM is technology that allows you to store information about your customers and prospects. For example, when someone makes a purchase with your company, the CRM creates a record for that person. It records whatever information you can capture about the customer (I'll discuss examples next) and then combines this information with the history of your relationship with the customer (this can include purchases, customer service interactions, marketing channels, etc.).

One of the largest CRM companies is Salesforce, which has CRM solutions that start at $25 a month.

MARKETING AUTOMATION

Marketing automation is similar to CRM, with the primary difference between the two being that marketing automation primarily stores and automates marketing data, versus the CRM that is focused on prospect or customer data. Thus, you might use your marketing automation tool to capture information about a new prospect and nurture that prospect by sending them marketing materials. At the point that the potential customer is valuable enough to be considered a sales prospect, the marketing automation system passes the customer information over to the CRM so that the sales team can close the deal.

HubSpot, Pardot, Mailchimp, Act-On, and Marketo are popular marketing automation systems. Some of these companies offer free starter versions that have minimal initial needs.

WEB ANALYTICS

Even if you don't run an e-commerce company, you probably still have a lot of visitors coming to your website. Web analytics software helps you capture how people are interacting with your website. This includes metrics like what pages they've visited, purchases, the most popular geographies and times of day when people come to your site, and whether your overall site traffic is increasing over time.

The most popular solution for web analytics is from Google: Google Analytics. Their basic package (which is very robust) is free to use. Another popular choice is Adobe Analytics, which does not offer a free product and is typically used by very large companies or companies that require a more sophisticated set in their data collection to solve specific business challenges that Google Analytics may not do well enough.

POINT-OF-SALE (POS) TRACKING

When you go to a retail store and make a purchase, a POS system collects information about that purchase. On one level, this information tells the retailer when inventory is getting low in that store. At a more advanced level, when a consumer enters their loyalty club information at the checkout, the POS can create a record of consumer purchases that can be used for future promotions. You can also leverage these systems to connect information about what users may have purchased from your website to garner a fuller picture of the consumer.

Some popular POS systems include Square, Intuit, and Shopify. Small business pricing starts at less than $100 a month.

CALL TRACKING

Call tracking is the technology used in the example at the beginning of this chapter: a system that collects information about phone calls coming into your call center. This can include understanding what marketing drove the call, the time of day or day of the week of the call, and whether the call resulted in a purchase.

CallRail, Dialog Tech, and RingDNA are three leading call solutions. Prices start at less than $50 a month for a basic package.

ADVERTISING NETWORKS REPORTING

When you buy advertising on an ad network, the ad network typically has a robust suite of reports available for you to evaluate. Online ad networks, like Google and Facebook, typically provide more data than offline networks, like Clear Channel (billboards) or TV networks. Nonetheless, all of these networks have plenty of data to share with you, and the reports are almost always free (but you pay for the advertising, of course).

CONSUMER SURVEYS

We've all visited a website and seen a pop-up asking us to share a few thoughts about our shopping experience or ordered a burrito and received an offer on the receipt promising us $5 off our next order if we answered some survey questions online. These are examples of consumer surveys. Savvy marketers use these to measure customer satisfaction and understand the needs of their customers better.

The most popular online consumer survey tool is Survey-Monkey, which offers an entirely free version (with limited functionality). There are also companies like Hotjar that allow you to survey active users on your site.

THIRD-PARTY SEGMENTATION

For better or worse, there are companies that collect trillions of data points about consumers and businesses and then sell this information to marketers. For example, the three credit reporting agencies (Experian, Equifax, and TransUnion) collect data from credit card purchases, home purchases, mortgages, and banks and allow marketers to enhance the existing data they have on their customers. These tools are typically very expensive and require an understanding of consumer privacy laws like GDPR, CAN-SPAM, and CCPA to properly use, so we consider this a tactic for advanced marketers only.

ENTERPRISE RESOURCE PLANNING (ERP) SOFTWARE

ERP software helps businesses manage many different back-office tasks through one program. Typically this starts with accounting, finance, and payroll and can also include inventory/warehousing, procurement, and reporting and analytics. Set up properly, ERP is the primary source of truth for what is going on in the business in terms of finance, product performance, and people management. ERP software is usually pretty expensive; the most basic package usually costs at least $1,000 a month.

ACCOUNTING SOFTWARE

For smaller businesses that can't afford and don't need an ERP, a basic accounting software package is usually good enough to run the business. Accounting software can keep track of all the financial aspects of the business: revenue, profit, costs, invoicing, payroll, taxes, etc. QuickBooks, a leader in this space, offers a robust solution for less than $50 a month.

A word of caution about any technology you are considering for your business: proper setup and training is crucial to success. While many technologies promise to be incredibly easy to use, the reality is that the best results often come only after hiring an expert to help with the initial implementation and staff training. One way to think of this is as shown in the graphic.

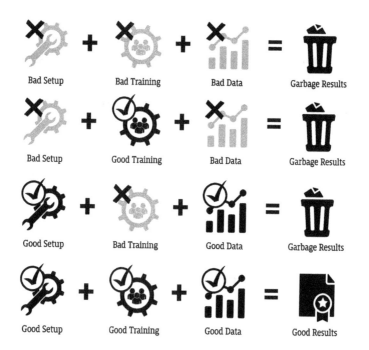

In other words, **the best, most valuable data in the world is worthless if the tool you are using to analyze it isn't working properly.** Imagine the Air Force with the fastest, most advanced fighter jets in the world deciding not to train their pilots. That's what happens when you buy great technology and don't invest in proper setup and training!

My point here is partly to encourage you to "do it right" from the beginning, but also to remind you to be aware that the total price tag of a piece of technology is never just the monthly fee that they charge you. Be prepared to invest in consultants as part of your technology adoption plan.

With that big caveat, let's jump into the four ways to gain an unfair data advantage over the competition. The four are:

1. Proprietary data
2. Better measurement
3. Connecting different pieces of data
4. Better analysis of data

UNFAIR DATA ADVANTAGE #1: PROPRIETARY DATA

Proprietary data is data that you have that your competitors do not. This is the most defendable type of unfair data advantage because your competitors will never have access to this data. It is your unique data.

Here's an example from my digital marketing agency, 3Q Digital. In 2019, we managed over $1.5 billion of advertising spend on Google and Facebook for our clients. For every dollar of advertising we spent, Google and Facebook provided us with around 25 data points—things like the geography of the person who clicked on the ad, the time of day, and whether that dollar resulted in a sale for our advertisers. Do the math: 1.5 billion × 25 = 37.5 billion pieces of information.

Other agencies—and, for that matter, individual advertisers—get the same data points from Google and Facebook, but their data set is much smaller than ours—usually between 100 and 1,000 times smaller. As a result, their data set is not as rich as ours. Where we may have 500 data points about a certain trend (perhaps "do people in North Dakota prefer Coke or Pepsi?"), a competitor may only have one or two data points and therefore be unable to draw a statistically significant conclusion ("statistically significant" means that there is enough data to mathematically conclude that the results are accurate).

My agency uses this data to learn how to improve the advertising campaigns of our clients. Of course, this benefits our clients because we can make changes to their campaigns that an agency with a smaller data set simply wouldn't have uncovered. And it also benefits the agency, because when a potential client is deciding between us and a smaller agency, we will often win because the client knows that our data advantage will simply drive better results for them.

Think about your business, and ask yourself two questions: Do I have data that no one else has? Are there types of data that I have much more of than my competitors? If you can answer either of these questions affirmatively, you have proprietary data.

To be clear, every company has proprietary data. If you only have one customer, you have proprietary data (you know what that customer bought, how much profit you made from them, and so on). If you have only made a dollar of revenue, you have proprietary data (you know how much profit you made off that dollar and which product was sold to drive that revenue). In other words, this is an area where every company has an opportunity to create an unfair marketing advantage.

To help you brainstorm the types of proprietary data you might have, here are some common areas where companies have proprietary data. Next to each of these types of proprietary data, fill in the box with one of three marks:

- If you know you currently have this data, put a check mark in the box.
- If you know that you definitely do not have this data and will never have it, put an X in the box.

- If you aren't sure if you have this data, or if you know you have it but you're not sure you can access it, put a question mark in the box.

The first type of proprietary data is customer information. This can include:

☐ Customer information (name, email address, home address, phone number)
☐ Professional information (company, role, job tenure, seniority)
☐ Demographic information about your customers (age, gender, location, family size, income)
☐ Psychographic information about your customers (hobbies, interests, attitudes, aspirations)
☐ Relationship with your company (what they've purchased from you, when they last purchased, how frequently they buy from you, the total revenue you've made from the customer, how they respond to your promotions)

The next type is behavioral information:

☐ What pages on your site have they viewed?
☐ How many times have they visited your site?
☐ How many transactions have they completed with your brand?
☐ What channels are responsible for driving users to your site most?

Another type is product information:

- Product sales (which products sell the most, which products are seeing sales growth or sales decline)
- Product profit
- Products that are bought together
- Product purchase behavior by location, date, online versus offline, consumer demographics

Financial information is another category of data you have access to:

- Company financial performance by time (time of day, day of week, monthly or quarterly)
- Product financial performance (which customers are most profitable, how much it costs to produce a product)
- Location financial performance (best-performing retail locations, profit by geography of customers)
- Pricing information (how much price impacts sales and profit, if customers respond to sales or coupons)
- Customer Lifetime Value (LTV) (how much on average your customer is spending with your company both historically and likely from future transactions)

Last and definitely not least is marketing information:

- Messaging and positioning (which messages are most

effective, how customers respond to different branding campaigns)
- ☐ Advertising (which advertising channels, publishers, or campaigns drive the most profit, how increasing or decreasing your advertising budget changes sales and profits)
- ☐ PR (which PR campaigns drive web visitors or increase sales)

To be clear, this is not an exhaustive list. Each of these lists could probably be 100 items long. The point is to show you the types of data you already have inside your company. As I said previously, most businesses don't lack data; they lack the ability to identify the valuable data and make it actionable.

CREATING YOUR LIST OF PROPRIETARY DATA

Take a moment and start to catalog the data you have. For each category you know you already have data about or feel confident you can start to get the data, work with your team to start creating a master list of your proprietary data. Depending on the category of data, you will likely have to talk to different people in your organization. For example, your finance team is best equipped to help you understand your proprietary financial data, while your marketing team is the best place to understand your marketing data.

Don't hand these teams a photocopied page of this book

and ask them if they have the five to 10 data point examples listed here. Instead, schedule a brainstorming meeting with them, and collectively try to come up with every minute point of data you can. There are no bad answers—just write down everything you can think of! The more you come up with (and the more granular each point is), the better. Note: you may even want to add data points to the list that you'd *like to have* but currently don't have access to—this can be a good reminder to later track down that data and add it in.

Once you've created your exhaustive list, open up Microsoft Excel or Google Sheets and start to describe these data points in more detail. Here are some sample columns you can use:

- Name of data point
- Type
- Description
- How could we use this data?
- Is it currently available?
- Where is it?
- Format
- Team that owns this data
- Priority

Ideally, you want each row to match one data point with one data source. For example, with Google Ads, you can get reporting about the geography, time of day, order size, and many other points. Make each of these a unique row in your document.

The sheet should look something like this:

Data Point	Type	Description	How Can We Use This Data to Improve Marketing?	Currently Available?	Where Is It?	Format	Team That Owns This	Priority
Google advertising spend	Marketing	Google gives us a report that can be broken down into daily data that shows clicks, costs, sales, and profit.	Optimize our Google advertising spend to only focus on campaigns that make us money.	Yes, 24/7	Google Reporting	Available as Excel document. We can also have it sent directly via an API if we want to build an advanced tool.	Marketing, but if we want to build the API, we need to work with Engineering.	High
Geography of clicks and sales	Marketing	Google can provide country, state, zip code, and metro area of every click, impression, and sale.	We can identify the best geographies—where do we get the most sales—and then increase our ad spend there.	Yes, 24/7	Google Reporting	Available as Excel document. We can also have it sent directly via an API if we want to build an advanced tool.	Marketing, but if we want to build the API, we need to work with Engineering.	High
Geography of clicks and sales	Marketing	Facebook can provide country, state, zip code, and metro area of every click, impression, and sale.	We can identify the best geographies—where do we get the most sales—and then increase our ad spend there.	Yes, 24/7	Facebook Reporting	Available as Excel document. We can also have it sent directly via an API if we want to build an advanced tool.	Marketing, but if we want to build the API, we need to work with Engineering.	High
Product sales	Product	Every product that we've sold, with price, unit cost, and profit.	Allocate our marketing budget to the products that actually make us money.	Yes	ERP	Online report, or we can get a daily email report in Excel.	ERP consultant needs to set up this recording for us.	High
Product inventory	Product	How much inventory we have of each product, by warehouse and by total count.	If we have excess inventory of specific products, we may want to create a sale and promote this sale through our advertising.	Yes	ERP	Online report, or we can get a daily email report in Excel.	ERP consultant needs to set up this recording for us.	High
Top-performing stores by quarter	Financial	Quarterly report that shows sales by every store. We can get this at a store level or by geographic regions.	Invest in local marketing campaigns for stores that are underperforming.	Yes	Point of sale (POS)	Online report, or we can get a daily email report in Excel.	Retail team.	High
Customer lifetime value (LTV)	Customer	A breakdown of the total revenue we've gotten from a customer.	Create a loyalty program that rewards (and encourages more purchases) from our top customers.	No	CRM	Not currently available, but we could create this.	CRM consultant needs to set up this reporting for us.	Medium

As you can see, once you've filled out this sheet, opportunities start to jump out at you. You start to realize that you have a lot of proprietary data, that a lot of it is already available to you, and that you can use it to improve your marketing.

At this point, don't overthink your data. It's tempting to start imagining how you might create crazy combinations of data, custom software to analyze the data, and automated systems that instantly make decisions based on your data. I'll discuss a lot of these concepts later in this chapter, but for now, remember two adages: don't let the perfect get in the way of the good, and mo' data, mo' problems!

One of the top reasons people fail to use their proprietary data is "analysis paralysis"—they go down a rabbit hole trying to create the perfect and most accurate data set and end up feeling overwhelmed and doing nothing with their data. Avoid this tendency, and instead start to look to your data for small but powerful wins. Ask simple questions that will generate simple and actionable answers. For example:

- Which TV show works better for me: CNN or Stephen Colbert?
- Which product makes me the most profit?
- Which state has the most profitable customers on Google? On Facebook?

- Do men or women make me more profit?
- Which day of the week is most profitable?
- Which of my paid media channels are most effective at driving new customers and transactions?

These are all questions that allow you to make immediate (and unfair) marketing decisions! Product A is my most profitable product; I should increase the marketing budget for that product. My most profitable customers are in Arizona; I should spend more marketing dollars there.

Over time, you will ask much more nuanced questions, but for now, just assume that your competition isn't asking any of these questions or collecting any of this data. Then, every time you capture one more data point and ask one more simple question, you have an unfair marketing advantage.

ADVANCED PROPRIETARY DATA

If you are a beginner or intermediate marketer, you can—and in fact should—skip this section! Trying to implement the techniques below will likely cause more confusion than value.

If you are an expert marketer, you are most likely already getting a lot of the proprietary data described earlier, and you've probably moved beyond asking simple, linear questions about the data.

Where I often see expert marketers struggle is with the collection and organization of data. While Excel reports are great for small data sets, being able to capture millions of data points with Excel is a recipe for failure.

As a result, I recommend investing in two core pieces of technology: APIs and a data warehouse. Let's discuss each briefly.

An API (application programming interface) is a computer-to-computer connection between your business and a third-party data source. For example, Google Ads allows advertisers to build an API connection that directly slurps up every piece of information in an advertiser's account and deposits it in the advertiser's database.

APIs can be leveraged alongside an Extract, Transform, Load (ETL) or data extraction platform to schedule a download of your data on a regular basis (often in the middle of the night) and can quickly download and store millions of rows of data.

APIs are ubiquitous today. A 2016 report suggested that more than 40 APIs were being launched every week, with more than 15,000 worldwide.[2] As a result, the odds are high

---

2   Art Anthony, "Tracking the Growth of the API Economy," *Nordic APIs*, April 18, 2016, https://nordicapis.com/tracking-the-growth-of-the-api-economy/.

that you can access a lot of your marketing, financial, and customer data from third parties via APIs.

Building an API connection requires engineers, and sadly, API connections often break, meaning that if you are not paying attention, your data might be inaccurate for hours or days if the connection isn't working. As a result, a whole industry of API middleware has emerged, making it easier for companies to use API connections without massive teams of engineers building and maintaining the APIs.

Just as there are thousands of APIs, there seem to be thousands of API middleware solutions. Google, Oracle, Dell, and Amazon all offer API connector software, and smaller specialists like MuleSoft and Segment.io have grown big businesses by making API management easier.

Later in this chapter, I'll discuss how many software companies have combined API connections with additional data scrubbing and analysis. For now, however, I'll keep this discussion simple: if you want to organize and activate proprietary data at scale, you'll need to build API connections. I recommend that you use an API middleware company and a data connection consultancy to make this happen.

The second piece of software you'll want to invest in is a data warehouse. A data warehouse is a piece of software (usually cloud-based) that allows you to store data from many different sources. This means you can capture all of your different marketing channels, CRM data, POS data, third-party enhanced data, and so on. Again, as an advanced marketer, you need to have instant access to data points across all of your data sources. It would be impracticable to log into Google to download information and then log into Salesforce, then into Experian, and so on.

A data warehouse—combined with your API middleware—creates a seamless data collection and storage system. It sets you up to ask multilayered questions using many different data points at once. Again, I recommend that before you start trying to ask complex questions, you exhaust your list of simple questions first. Over time, however, you will want to start asking more nuanced questions, and the combination of APIs and a data warehouse enable this for your business.

Marketers typically choose data warehouses based on a combination of speed (how fast can you get data out of the system?), scale (can it handle a huge set of data?), and price (usually a combination of consulting fees to set up the data warehouse and a fee based on the amount of data you use). Leading data warehouses include Snowflake, Amazon Red-Shift, and Cloudera.

As with APIs, engineering support is required to get your data warehouse up and running. The data warehouse providers know this, which is why a consulting contract is typically required when signing up for the service, and—as mentioned—API middleware exists in part because most companies can't afford dedicated engineering to manage all of their APIs.

That said, even with API software and the consulting team at the data warehouse, you still need to have some engineers internally to interface with your software providers and make sure the setup works for your company.

A CASE STUDY ON PROPRIETARY DATA: WHEN YOUR LOCAL STORE KNOWS YOUR DAUGHTER IS PREGNANT BEFORE YOU DO

Target captures a lot of data about its customers. *The New York Times* summarized Target's incredible data collection efforts like this[3]:

> Target assigns each shopper a unique code—known internally as the Guest ID number—that keeps tabs on everything they buy. "If you use a credit card or a coupon, or fill out a survey, or mail in a refund, or call the customer help line, or open an email we've sent you or visit our website, we'll record it and link it to your Guest ID"...

---

3   Charles Duhigg, "How Companies Learn Your Secrets," *The New York Times*, February 16, 2012, https://www.nytimes.com/2012/02/19/magazine/shopping-habits.html?pagewanted=1&_r=1&hp.

Also linked to your Guest ID is demographic information like your age, whether you are married and have kids, which part of town you live in, how long it takes you to drive to the store, your estimated salary, whether you've moved recently, what credit cards you carry in your wallet and what websites you visit. Target can buy data about your ethnicity, job history, the magazines you read, if you've ever declared bankruptcy or got divorced, the year you bought (or lost) your house, where you went to college, what kinds of topics you talk about online, whether you prefer certain brands of coffee, paper towels, cereal, or applesauce, your political leanings, reading habits, charitable giving, and the number of cars you own.

No doubt the data scientists at Target love sifting through this data, looking for an unfair advantage. As *The Times* reports, one of the key segments of users Target wants to win is newly pregnant moms. Expecting moms need to buy a lot of stuff over the course of their pregnancy and parenthood. Getting those moms to choose Target over a competitor can drive years of revenue. So Target created a "pregnancy prediction score" based on the products that customer was purchasing at Target (proprietary data!).

Among the top indicators of pregnancy were unscented body lotion and supplements like calcium, zinc, and magnesium. Based on these purchases, Target would calculate the likelihood of pregnancy and send the customer "coupons timed to very specific stages of her pregnancy."

And here's where it gets weird. *The Times* shares this anecdote:

> About a year after [Target] created [its] pregnancy-prediction
> model, a man walked into a Target outside Minneapolis and
> demanded to see the manager. He was clutching coupons that
> had been sent to his daughter, and he was angry, according to
> an employee who participated in the conversation.
>
> "My daughter got this in the mail!" he said. "She's still in high school,
> and you're sending her coupons for baby clothes and cribs? Are
> you trying to encourage her to get pregnant?"
>
> The manager didn't have any idea what the man was talking
> about. He looked at the mailer. Sure enough, it was addressed to
> the man's daughter and contained advertisements for maternity
> clothing, nursery furniture, and pictures of smiling infants. The
> manager apologized and then called a few days later to apolo-
> gize again.
>
> On the phone, though, the father was somewhat abashed. "I had
> a talk with my daughter," he said. "It turns out there's been some
> activities in my house I haven't been completely aware of. She's
> due in August. I owe you an apology."

There are definitely concerning aspects to this story—Target
got a lot of bad publicity after its release, with allegations of
privacy violations (all the data is anonymized) and a breach
of trust with its customers. And Target actually dialed back

some of this targeting prior to the story's release. One of the lessons here is to understand the ethics of your proprietary data: there's an important difference between what you *could* do with your data and what you *should* do with your data.

With the proper ethical constraints, however, this is a clear example of an unfair data advantage!

CONCLUDING THOUGHTS ON PROPRIETARY DATA

Hopefully at this point, you realize that you have a lot of proprietary data inside your business and that if you ask simple questions about this data, you will uncover learnings that will benefit your business. To be clear, you don't have to be Walmart, Target, or Amazon to have access to unfair proprietary data.

While it is true that having more data than someone else is often an advantage, even the smallest business has unique information that—if used properly—will create an unfair data advantage. Identifying this proprietary data and then using it to improve your marketing is all you need to do to get a leg up on most of the competition!

UNFAIR DATA ADVANTAGE #2: BETTER TRACKING AND MEASUREMENT

Imagine going into a tailor and asking him to measure you

for a new set of pants. The tailor takes out some measuring tape, but the smallest denomination of measurement is one yard (three feet). So the tailor measures your legs and says, "Looks like your pants are going to be a yard long, with a waist of a yard wide."

Of course, unless you are SpongeBob SquarePants, these pants will not fit very well. We expect tailors to be much more granular than that. Tailors will measure in fractions of inches, so you might end up with pants that are 36.25 inches long with a 28.5-inch waist.

Shockingly, when it comes to measuring business data, many companies take the yardstick approach and end up with vague and unusable information. Go back to the first example I discussed: simply understanding the difference in performance between two different TV shows can be the difference between success and failure in your marketing. Suffice to say, if you can measure your data at a more accurate and granular level than the competition, it will create an unfair marketing advantage.

HOW TO TRACK YOUR DATA

I've discussed the most common places where you can find your data, such as your CRM system, POS software, or advertising partners. All of these systems have tons of data that can give you a marketing advantage. Most of these systems, however, aren't set up out of the box to provide detailed measurement of your marketing. To make that happen, you need to set up tracking.

Tracking, simply put, is any system you set up to collect data. For example, the different toll-free numbers we used to figure out which TV show worked best are a form of tracking. Companies that set up accurate tracking have an advantage over companies that don't track their data, or don't do it accurately, because they can make better decisions based on data.

Again, with data, it is easy to get overwhelmed with complexity and give up. For this reason, I recommend starting with tracking basics, mastering these, and then moving on to more advanced techniques (which I'll discuss in a separate section later on). Remember that many of your competitors aren't even doing the basics, so just setting up a foundation gives you a marketing advantage.

As you read this section, it may be helpful to try to visualize how all of these pieces of data come together. A colleague of mine recommends developing a "systems and data model." Identify the KPIs and objectives and the primary data creation and collecting systems, and then create the data model detailing how each system will be joined together. This can be done in PowerPoint and is a handy way of trying to keep track of how the different data sources, software, and business objectives should eventually come together to help your business.

If that last paragraph felt overwhelming to you, you are not alone! To be clear, setting up tracking and your overall model is something that is best left to an expert. Even the most basic tracking usually requires some programming knowledge. So this section will not go into detail about the process of setting up tracking and will assume that you will be working with an experienced professional to get you started.

With that in mind, I recommend focusing on these five forms of tracking: customer ID/login, cookies, tracking URLs, phone numbers, and coupon codes. I'll review each separately.

Customer ID/Login

When a customer purchases something from a business (or even signs up for a newsletter), businesses almost always assign that customer a unique identifier, if only to make sure that the order is properly fulfilled. For online purchases, the user is often asked to register for the site with a login ID and a password. For offline purchases, the customer's mailing address combined with their name is the unique identifier.

This information is usually captured in your CRM, an online

shopping platform like Shopify or Magento, or (for retail stores) your POS system.

Customer ID is highly valued tracking data because it is considered deterministic and not probabilistic, meaning that the data is known to be true rather than inferred to be true. In other words, when someone places an order and that information is entered into your CRM system, you have near 100 percent confidence that this order actually occurred, barring some sort of computer error or fraud. Other forms of tracking that I'll discuss have much lower levels of confidence.

The key to tracking a customer ID is to continually find ways to "append" (add) new pieces of data to the customer ID. Most CRM systems, for example, will readily capture name, address, phone number, and other basic information about a customer but won't automatically connect purchase information, marketing interactions, or third-party psycho-graphic profiling to the customer ID.

The more you can connect the dots between your customer ID and every interaction that customer has had with your business, the more powerful the data becomes. As such, whether you are capturing a customer ID offline or online, and whether you are a consumer-facing (B2C) or business-facing (B2B) business, you need to set up a customer ID system that:

- Stores a unique record for every customer who purchases from or interacts with your business.
- Modifies the out-of-the-box tracking from your CRM, commerce platform, or POS to allow each unique record to be appended.
- Identifies and appends sources of data that will enhance your customer IDs—this includes marketing, financial, and product data.

To show you an example of how this might work, assume you are advertising on Facebook, and a consumer clicks on your ad (which costs you $2 in advertising). The ad encourages the user to sign up for your email newsletter, which the consumer does. A few weeks later, after getting sent 10 emails, the consumer decides to buy something for $50. Then, over the course of the next year, the consumer spends $500 with your business.

Your CRM system—out of the box—would only know that you have a new customer ID—the person who signed up for the newsletter. Similarly, your Shopify system would only know that someone made a purchase, and Facebook would only know that you spent $2 on an ad with a return of only $50.

If you set up your CRM tracking properly around this unique customer ID, however, all of this information can be accessed inside your CRM system. You can connect

Facebook and Shopify to your CRM such that cost and revenue at the customer level can be stored in the CRM. This gives you two huge advantages: first, you get a much better understanding of the individual customer. You can customize offers to this customer or provide VIP service because you have a complete history of the customer's interactions with your business. Second, you can start to aggregate data across many customers. For example, you can run a report of all customer IDs who clicked on Facebook ads. Do they spend more or less than people who click on Google ads?

Cookies

Whenever you visit a new website, you'll typically see a notice somewhere on the page that reads like this:

This website uses cookies

We use cookies to personalize content and ads, to provide social media features, and to analyze our traffic. We also share information about your use of our site with our social media, advertising, and analytics partners who may combine it with other information that you've provided to them or that they've collected from your use of their services.

A cookie is a storage mechanism for data and information that is collected by a website when someone visits their site. Typically this includes a user's anonymous or known user ID, visit number, customer type, and other information that a company may want to store for tracking or site functionality that they may need to leverage at a later point in time.

All of this is incredibly valuable to you, the business owner. For example, if you want to track whether or not a visitor to your site is a returning visitor or use an identifier of a customer type to show the user a different offer in your homepage hero ad space, you can do that by leveraging cookies, as well as use the values stored in the cookies to pass this information to your web analytics software to let you make smart decisions about your website. Note: Google has announced that it will no longer allow third-party cookies to be used to track customers using its popular Google Chrome browser by 2022 at the latest. This decision has been met with strong opposition from the advertising community, which sees this as a way for Google to keep data to itself (and thus hurt smaller companies that don't have this unfair advantage!). It is supported by privacy advocates, who think that cookies store too much personal information about consumers. No doubt, there will be a lot of back and forth on this topic in the next few years, so stay tuned!

PRIVACY POLICIES, GDPR, AND CCPA

You may be asking: why do websites keep telling me that they use cookies? Is it some altruistic desire to keep consumers informed about their privacy? Sadly, no! In the last few years, two laws have been passed—one in Europe and one in California—that have required websites to be much more transparent about how they use a consumer's information. The European law is called GDPR for short; the California law is CCPA.

While the laws differ, in some ways quite significantly, the primary objective of each law is the same: inform consumers of how their personal data is being used, require websites to take reasonable efforts to protect consumer data, and give consumers options for how their data is used.

Nothing in this book should be taken as legal advice, and I'm not about to try to explain to you the nuances of GDPR and CCPA. As such, my best advice is to seek legal advice from an attorney with experience in GDPR and CCPA who will help you understand what sort of disclosures you need to make to consumers and how you can still collect data without running into legal problems. That attorney will probably also guide you on how to properly set up your privacy policy and terms and conditions for use of your website—you'll notice that every site you visit also has these sections at the bottom of the page.

Tracking URL Parameters

Tracking URL parameters are custom URL values that you can create to capture data about a user that is not captured in a cookie. For example, let's say you are running a special promotional message in your ads on YouTube letting users know that you have a 25 percent off sale in December. A cookie has no way of knowing that your ad has this message, but you can create a unique URL that will let your web analytics package know that this message was seen by the visitor.

If your regular URL is www.3QDigital.com, the tracking URL might look like this: www.3QDigital.com/?ad=December+Sale. When you later look in Google Analytics, you'll see that there's reporting for a page called "December Sale."

Note: this is another example of combining two types of tracking to get superior results. Earlier, I noted that enhancing your standard CRM reporting with marketing or financial information not typically captured by the CRM system will give you better insights. In this case, we enhanced standard cookie tracking with a tracking URL.

As you get more advanced, you can start to layer enhancement on top of enhancement. Imagine, for example, if you combine your cookie data and tracking URL data with the customer ID data you are storing in your CRM. You will start to see how you can get data that your inexperienced competitors could never even imagine!

Phone Numbers

As shown by the example of tracking two different TV shows, creating unique phone numbers to track different marketing campaigns is a great way to get better data. As noted earlier in the book, call tracking software today is very sophisticated in terms of what it can measure.

These systems also have the capability of setting up "dynamic phone numbers," meaning that the system can automatically create a toll-free number on the fly, enabling you to track hundreds of different marketing campaigns at once (theoretically, if you had 1,000 marketing campaigns running, you could track all of them with a unique, dynamically created phone number, giving you the ability to connect phone sales back to the channel, campaign, or even specific ad that you ran). Note that this works equally well with your website or online ads, where you can serve a dynamic phone number digitally and then connect your cookie data to your phone tracking data.

Coupon Codes

We've all received a piece of direct mail with a message on it that says something like, "Enter 'SAVE20NOW' on our website to save 20 percent today." Sometimes these ads encourage the consumer to bring the flyer into the physical store. Savvy marketers create unique coupon codes to try to measure the effectiveness of different marketing approaches. So, for example, they may test two different marketing messages on their direct mail campaign and create two different codes—one might say "SAVE2oNOW," and another might say, "2oPERCENTOFF."

Coupon codes can be used in direct mail, radio, and TV campaigns, on the web, in email—pretty much anywhere! Again, where you can connect this with other forms of tracking, you can create much better reporting. For example, if someone clicks a link to save 20 percent on your website, you can make this link a tracking URL and record additional data about the user beyond the cookie information.

THE IMPORTANCE OF DATA GRANULARITY

Peter Drucker said, "If you can't measure it, you can't improve it." He could have also said, "The more granularly you measure something, the more you can improve it."

Imagine you have 1,000 customers for your business. The average customer spends $100 with you over their lifetime. That's certainly useful information, and you can use this to figure out how much you should spend to acquire a new customer (it should probably be less than $100!). But you could analyze your customers at a much more granular level. For example, what if you knew that:

· Men spend $80, and women spend $120.

- People in Florida spend $50, and people in Iowa spend $200.
- People who call in via the toll-free number spend two times as much as people who order online.
- People who buy in December spend $75, and people who buy in May spend $300.

You could also take this data and find really granular details, like:

- Women in Florida who buy in December spend $250, but women in Florida who buy in March spend $50, unless they use a credit card, in which case they spend $200.

As you get into these nuances of customer behavior, you start to see that getting "average" values is not nearly as valuable as getting very precise, granular information. So it goes without saying that setting up granular tracking is really important.

Knowing what you want to track is an inexact science. It starts with educated guesses, and then, as you start to use the data, it becomes more refined. The good news for you is that I've already helped you create these educated guesses. In the prior section, when you identified all the pieces of proprietary data you had (customers, financial, marketing, and product), you were also creating a list of granular metrics you could be tracking. In other words, if you identified "month of purchase" as a piece of proprietary data, that's probably something you will want to start tracking.

The caveat here is, once again, this warning: **don't let the perfect get in the way of the good.** For example, let's say that you think the geography of your customers is an important metric you want to track. When we think about geography, we can go very broad or very granular. For example:

- Continent
- Country
- State
- City
- Zip code
- Zip code +4
- Neighborhood
- Street address

If you are Lockheed Martin and you are selling advanced satellite systems to national governments, it doesn't really matter if your order came from zip code 94402 or zip code 94403. You probably only have 1,000 customers in the world anyway, and you probably know them all on a first-name basis. So you'd be wasting your time if you started tracking granular geography. On the other hand, if you are Pizza Hut, you might want to know exactly where an order is coming from—even at the street address level if possible. You could use this information to follow up an order with some coupons via mail and optimize your delivery drivers based on the density of orders.

The other factor to consider is data density—whether the data would even be credible if you could get it at a granular level. Again, if Lockheed sells 10 satellite systems a year, knowing the city of each purchase is probably not going to be very valuable to them because the data is not statistically significant. Put another way, they may get one order from Chicago this year, but they got zero orders over the prior 10 years. Should they double down on Chicago (it did drive 10 percent of their sales this year), or should they save their money because historically they've never gotten anything out of Chicago?

The answer is most likely: this is an irrelevant question because there is not enough data to draw an inference. Even trying to measure performance at this level creates more confusion than value. They should instead leverage an account-based marketing approach to target their specific customers to get outcomes.

Be realistic about what you are trying to granularly measure: try to only measure at the level of granularity where it can help you make smart marketing decisions, and you have enough data to get statistically significant results.

WHAT IS STATISTICAL SIGNIFICANCE, EXACTLY?

If you went to Las Vegas, put a quarter in a slot machine, and won $1 million , you could come to one of two conclusions: first, slot machines pay out 4 million times whatever your investment is, or second, you were incredibly lucky. Instinctively, we understand that the second conclusion is the correct one because we know that most people lose money on slot machines.

Now imagine that instead of playing a quarter one time, you played that same machine 1 million times, and for your $250,000 investment (a quarter times 1 million), you ended up getting $225,000 back. With that large sample size of data, you could come to a much more accurate conclusion: the machine pays back 90 cents for every dollar invested.

The more data you have, the more confidence you have in the accuracy of the data. Statisticians use the term "statistical significance" to describe results that are highly likely to be true (usually a level of confidence of 95 percent or higher) instead of the result of sampling error.

Today, there are free calculators online that you can use to determine statistical significance. You don't need to measure the statistical significance of every set of data you analyze. Often you will have so much data that you won't need to formally measure the statistical significance to know the data is

If you've properly set up all of your different data sources (CRM, POS, web analytics, etc.) and tracking tools (cookies, customer ID, advertising data, etc.), you have the foundation to start to do granular data analysis and discover learnings that can give you an unfair advantage.

So now the big question: where do you start? The answer is different for every business. That said, **here's an overarching theory that will help you figure out the right path for you:** *look for differences in data.*

Recall that I've mentioned several times how finding averages across your marketing is often a mistake because it results in overpaying for bad customers and underpaying (undermarketing!) to good customers. Finding differences in data is the antithesis of finding averages. You are actively looking for granular segments of your data that jump out at you and say, "Treat me differently!"

Remember, the more granular you can get, the better. So while it is great to know that people in Arizona buy more than people in Nevada, it's even better to know that people in Phoenix buy more than people in Tempe, that people in Phoenix who click on a Google ad buy more than people who click on a Facebook ad, and that people in Phoenix who click on a Google ad on their iPhone buy more than people who click on a Google ad on their Android phone. As long as you have statistical significance, you can keep drilling further and further into more granularity.

One way to think of this is to create a bingo card with all the different ways you can measure your company's performance. Along each axis of the card, you might create labels like geography, time, advertising source, product, demographics, and so on.

Now start to combine these data types, and see if interesting differences are created (for those of you who have played the board game Clue, this will sound familiar). So you might try:

- Do men (demographics) in Arizona (geography) buy more blue widgets or red widgets (product) in winter or spring (time)?
- What's my profit (financial) on blue widgets (product) on Google (advertising source) from people who are married (demographics)?
- How many visits (behavioral) does it take for men (demographics) in Phoenix (geography) using Google Search (advertising source) to buy blue widgets (product)?

Remember: for each of these measurements, you have a constraint and an opportunity. The constraint is statistical significance. You need to make sure you are capturing enough data to be confident that the results are accurate. The opportunity is granularity: the more you can drill down into micro-findings, the more you can outflank the competition.

If you think about it, **the right level of granularity is the most microscopic result you can get that is still statistically significant.** So, again, if you can move from Arizona to Phoenix and then from Phoenix to a specific zip code in Phoenix and still get statistical significance, you should do it.

Three other important caveats: first, don't get too hung up on statistical significance. What I mean by this is that you don't need to hire a full-time statistician to join your team and bless every analysis you do as statistically accurate. For a lot of reports that you run, it will be more than clear that the sample size is large enough to make smart decisions. If, for example, you have 1,000 purchases in Arizona and 1,000 purchases in New York and you see a 40 percent difference in purchase size between the two states, even if the difference would be 35 percent if you got a bigger sample size, you clearly have enough data to make a decision and treat the two states differently.

Second, to slightly contradict a prior statement, sometimes

too much granularity is a waste of time because you can't act on the data. For example, let's say that you discovered that people who drove past your billboards in the morning were 10 times more likely to buy your products than people who drove past them in the afternoon. Given that billboards can only be bought on a monthly basis, what good would it do for you to know this? It may be a fun fact, but you can't create an unfair marketing advantage as a result, so it is largely a waste of time (and yes, it may be true that this information could be useful for a digital billboard purchase or for other parts of your marketing, but let's not overthink the point here).

Lastly, there is still plenty of value in non-granular data when a granular report isn't statistically significant. If you don't have enough data to figure out geographic performance at a city level, zoom out and look at the state level. If you can't determine time-of-day performance, look at day-of-week performance.

The bottom line is this: you have a lot of data, and if you can find the right granular slices of this data to analyze, you can start to see differences in the data that your competitors can't. Don't overthink this. Just start assembling different combinations of data, zooming in and out, assessing statistical significance (or just trusting your gut), and looking for opportunities to optimize. Remember that most of your competitors don't know how to access their data at all, and others are frozen with analysis paralysis, looking for the absolute 100 percent accurate finding before they make a change. You can give yourself an unfair data advantage by overcoming both of these problems now!

UNFAIR DATA ADVANTAGE #3: CONNECTING DATA

A lot of the techniques I am talking about in this chapter can be layered on top of each other. Once you've identified your proprietary data, the next step is to set up tracking. Once you've set up tracking, the next step is to create granular reports that show differences in data. I've purposely designed this chapter to start with the basic tenets of an unfair data advantage and progressively move into the more complex aspects.

To reiterate an important point here: you can—and should—start creating unfair advantages even if you haven't implemented every advanced technique that I've described. With that in mind, this section is definitely a lot more advanced than prior sections, so it is 100 percent okay to either skip it or decide to hold off on trying to implement the ideas herein.

Two of the biggest challenges with data are normalization and attribution. Let's briefly explain what both of these terms mean. Normalization is taking different sets of data and establishing commonality between them. For example, if Customer 105 sees a TV commercial and calls the toll-free number but decides not to order, and then the next day Customer 105 clicks on a Google ad, visits the website, and converts, unless these two systems (the call center and the online checkout) are connected, there's no way to understand the complete journey that this customer took on his way to making a purchase.

Suffice to say, the more you can connect disparate data sources, the more you can make informed decisions about your marketing. Remember that bad data plus a good measurement system still results in bad results!

Once you've normalized the data, you can then think about attribution. Attribution is a methodology that gives proportional credit to different touchpoints on the way to a purchase. In the previous example, should the phone call get 50 percent credit for the sale, 100 percent credit, zero percent credit, or something else? Obviously, the amount of credit the call gets will greatly influence whether you conclude that your call center is vital or worthless to your business's success.

NORMALIZATION 101

The key to normalization is to create unified viewpoints where you can see different pieces of information together. I've actually already talked about several pieces of technology that are designed to accomplish this for your business for specific sets of information. For example:

- Your CRM system captures everything you know about your customers.
- Your web analytics system captures everything you know about your website traffic.
- Your ERP system captures everything you know about finances and product sales.

As noted, however, these systems are not set up to provide out-of-the-box unified viewpoints—they need to be set up to do this. The other important note about these systems is that they are each designed to provide a different perspective on your data. The CRM system is designed to tell you about your customers, whereas the ERP is designed to tell you about your products. As such, if you try to use your CRM system to normalize product data or your ERP system to normalize customer data, you will likely fail.

The solution: normalize different data in different systems. Use CRM data to make your product view in the ERP better, and use product-level data to make the customer data in the CRM better.

The key to doing any of this is creating unique identifiers at a granular level so that you can match data from one system to another. Let's walk through how this might work. Let's say that you have a customer who has the customer ID 012345, and let's say that this customer clicked on the keyword "best blue widgets" on Google and subsequently bought a product with the product ID AAA123.

Your out-of-the-box CRM system is set up to capture the customer ID but is not set up to record how the customer found you or what product they bought. You can solve both of these problems. In your CRM, whenever a new file is created, you have your engineers create two custom fields, one called "marketing source" and the other called "product."

When the customer clicks on your Google ad, you create a special tracking URL that records the keyword that the customer clicked. Perhaps it looks like this: www.bluewidgets.com/?keyword=best+blue+widgets. This tracking URL value gets recorded and persists with the customer as they shop your website. So if they eventually make a purchase, the commerce platform can capture the source of the traffic.

You can then set up a feed between your commerce platform and the CRM that sends the marketing source information into the CRM and matches it with the customer ID of the customer. You establish a similar feed between your ERP and CRM, this time sending the product information.

Again, the trick here is to create unique identifiers that connect different sets of information. Connecting the dots allows for the advanced data analysis that gives you an unfair advantage. How you do this is up to you and your engineering team—in the previous example, we used a tracking URL and a custom field in your CRM; your engineering team may like this approach or want to use a different method. The most important thing is that you just get it done!

ADVANCED NORMALIZATION: DMPS AND CDPS

Given the unfair advantage marketers can achieve through better normalization of data, it's not surprising that many technology companies have built solutions designed to help companies with their data normalization. Currently, there are two tech solutions that marketers use to improve their normalization: DMPs and CDPs.

These tools are not cheap (typically at least $5,000 per month for the most basic implementation), and they really only benefit companies that have already spent a lot of engineering resources tracking and collecting their data. For this reason, I don't recommend considering either software package until you feel confident that you have covered all the basics described in this chapter.

Let's start with basic definitions. DMP stands for data management platform, and CDP stands for customer data platform. Here's the unique value in each of these solutions:

- **DMP:** DMPs are primarily used to collect, aggregate, and normalize behavioral and media exposure data. They also enable you to layer third-party data—such as psychographic data that you buy from a credit reporting agency—and start to run analysis that can improve your business. DMPs specialize in collecting anonymized data about users via cookies (see separate discussion on this topic). Leading DMPs include Adobe Audience Manager, Krux (now owned by Salesforce), BlueKai (owned by Oracle), and Lotame.
- **CDP:** The primary advantage of a CDP is that it can handle known data about a customer. For example, if you have personally identifiable information (PII) about your customers, such as name, address, and credit card information, a CDP can help you interpret this data while maintaining the confidentiality of the PII. CDPs do not collect cookie data like DMPs. Top CDPs include Segment, TreasureData, Lattice Engines, and Tealium.

Given the fact that CDPs collect first-party data and DMPs don't, you might conclude that CDPs are obviously better than DMPs, but the choice is not so clear. There are really three factors to consider when choosing among these solutions:

- **Use Case:** If you are primarily interested in evaluating your advertising spend, a DMP will do a great job of normalizing this data and giving you great insights.

CDPs are more complex to set up than DMPs, so buying something with features that will take time to implement but that you will never actually use increases the risk of implementation failure and wastes engineers' time. By contrast, if you are looking to measure a customer life cycle and really understand how individual customers interact with your business, a CDP is a necessity because of its ability to handle PII.

- **Data Security and Privacy**: Anytime you are capturing PII, you need to be keenly aware of the legal consequences of a data breach. For example, GDPR has fines as high as 20 million euros or 4 percent of your revenue (whichever is greater) for egregious data breaches. Now, to be clear, it's very unlikely for most companies, especially small businesses, to be fined at this sort of level, but even without fines, data breaches lead to really bad PR and potential class-action lawsuits. Put another way, you should always think twice about the PII you capture and, for that matter, whether you want to use a third-party tool like a CDP to retain this data. In the event of a breach, it will be your company, not the CDP, that suffers the most damage.

- **Price**: As a general rule, the more features a tool offers, the more it costs, both for the subscription and for the implementation and maintenance. CDPs are able to handle higher privacy risks than DMPs, so they cost more than DMPs. I often tell clients that they don't need a Ferrari if all they are doing is driving a mile to the supermarket every day.

ATTRIBUTION

Imagine getting a call from a potential customer. You ask the customer, "How did you find out about us?" and she responds, "I typed your company name into Google and found your telephone number." *Great*, you think. *This proves that having my company show up high in Google drives results. I need to double down on my investment in Google advertising and search engine optimization* (SEO).

But let's think about this in a little more detail: the customer typed your brand name into Google. How did they know to type in your name? No one wakes up in the morning and thinks, "I wonder if there is a company called [insert your company name] that does [insert your business offering]—I'm going to type that into Google and find out!" Instead, prior to that search on Google, the customer had to have learned about your company through some other source. Indeed, by the time they decided to do a search on Google, they had already decided they wanted to use your services. So really, how much credit for this customer does Google deserve?

This is the sort of question that attribution tries to answer. In most cases, someone who becomes a customer of your business has had multiple interactions (touchpoints) with your brand before they buy. This can include marketing channels like Google or direct mail, customer recommendations, news stories, PR, foot traffic in front of your store, and so on. How you allocate credit to each source can make a huge difference in how you invest your marketing dollars and the return you get as a result.

Let's go back to the prior example, where the person did a search for your brand name on Google. If you also knew that 10 seconds before they did that search, they saw one of your TV ads, would that change the way you value this search? Most reasonable people would conclude that the TV ad did all the heavy lifting and the Google search deserved little, if any, credit.

Thus, successful attribution is a two-step process: first, it's a matter of normalizing the data—making sure that whatever touchpoints a customer uses to connect with your brand are captured and connected. Second, attribution needs to give the right amount of credit to each touchpoint.

I've discussed normalization previously. As much as possible, your goal should be to create unified data such that you can connect every touchpoint to a customer or a conversion. On the second point—giving proper credit—there are generally three methods of attribution you can use:

- **Last-touch attribution:** The last touchpoint gets 100 percent of the credit.
- **First-touch attribution:** The first touchpoint gets 100 percent of the credit.
- **Multi-touch attribution (MTA):** A data-driven model is used to weigh the impact of each touchpoint in a user journey and across user journeys to appropriate the credit of each channel's influence on driving user conversions.

Before I discuss the pros and cons of each of these methods, it's worth stating that none of these models is perfect. In other words, whatever model you choose, you will not be 100 percent confident that the data is flawless. **Remember: don't let the perfect get in the way of the good.** Whatever attribution model you use, you will inevitably see results that make you question the model. As Winston Churchill once quipped, "Democracy is the worst form of Government except for all those other forms that have been tried from time to time." Such is the case with attribution models—they never seem great, but they are better than doing nothing.

With that in mind, let's review the three models.

Last-Touch Attribution

Last-touch attribution is a model that has two big advantages: it is simple, and it gives credit to the touch that directly leads to a purchase. When you use a last-touch model, you don't have to look at days or weeks of historical touchpoints to uncover the true source of a conversion. You just have to ask: what did the customer do before they bought from me? In most cases, whatever that touchpoint was, it is valuable to your business because it drove a sale.

The problem with last touch is that it often gives credit to a touchpoint that did little, if any, of the heavy lifting. I discussed the example of a person doing a search on Google for your brand. Obviously something drove that user's decision to do that search. A similar situation arises with coupons. If a customer brings in a coupon (let's say perhaps that was mailed to them via direct mail), did the coupon drive the customer to the store, or was the customer going to come in anyway and the coupon is now just costing you money (you are giving a discount to a customer who was going to buy from you regardless)?

As a general rule, last-touch attribution is a "better than nothing" model. In other words, while it benefits from simplicity, it generally gives too much credit to a touch that was not the primary driver of the sale. As a starting point, it is better than no attribution, but it has questionable accuracy.

First-Touch Attribution

Like last-touch attribution, first touch is also relatively

simple—you just need to isolate the first time a customer ever interacted with your brand. This is not as simple as last touch, however, because the time from first touch to conversion is sometimes measured in months or even years. So to get first touch right, you have to normalize data over a large time range (and you have to put a line in the sand: how far back in the past are we going to search for a touchpoint?). The strength of first touch is that the first interaction with your brand is obviously very important. This touch created awareness of your business and drove the customer down a path that eventually led to a purchase. But for this touch-point, the customer would have never even heard of your business.

The downside here is assuming that the first touch is the only important touchpoint to consider. For example, let's say that you are selling a very expensive enterprise software package. The first touch is an advertisement the customer sees at an airport, followed by an interaction at a trade show, a news story, a downloaded white paper, a meeting with the sales team, and eventually a purchase. The initial ad might have made it more likely for the customer to stop by the trade-show booth, but clearly there were a ton of sales and marketing touchpoints that made this eventual sale possible.

First-touch attribution is valuable for companies that have very little brand recognition and have a relatively short conversion path. Because the brand isn't well known, you can make an assumption that the initial interaction was incredibly valuable in driving the sale, especially if there are few touchpoints in a short time period after the first touch.

Multi-Touch Attribution (MTA)

Unlike first-touch and last-touch attribution, MTA is complex by design. The point of MTA is to try to weigh many different touchpoints across a long time period with as many marketing sources as possible. There are several different MTA models you can choose from:

- **Last-touch preferred:** gives the most weight to the last touch.
- **First-touch preferred:** gives the most weight to the first touch.
- **Even attribution:** gives even weight to all touches.
- **Algorithmic attribution:** uses data science to build a custom and potentially dynamic model.

The advantage of MTA is that the models have more shades of gray than a last-touch-only or first-touch-only model. This is especially true of the algorithmic MTA models, which can literally change the amount of credit a given touchpoint gets as it collects more data.

The biggest problem with MTA is its complexity. Very few

companies—even giant multinational firms—have the resources to hire data scientists to build MTA systems and analyze and validate the outputs. As such, to use an MTA model, you need to work with a third-party software provider and likely hire outside consultants to set up MTA properly.

A few of the leading MTA companies include:

- Visual IQ (now part of Nielsen)
- Markettime (now Neustar)
- Adobe
- Adometry (now Google)
- C3 Metrics

THE UNFAIR NORMALIZATION AND ATTRIBUTION ADVANTAGE

As with all data advantages, normalization and attribution give you an unfair advantage because you can more easily spot differences in the data.

By simply starting to go down the path of normalizing your data and trying to come up with proper attribution, you are already giving your business an advantage. Even the most basic setup will give you insight that a competitor who hasn't taken this step can't get. Remember, analysis paralysis is a real threat here. Many well-intentioned marketers get overwhelmed by the idea of connecting and attributing data, to the point that they never do anything at all. If you are okay with "good enough," you will see your marketing campaigns improve while your competitors that are obsessed with perfection remain stuck in place.

There are a million ways to benefit from normalized and attributed data, so it's impossible to create an exhaustive list. That said, here are a few high-level use cases that can make this data valuable to your business.

Look-Alike Modeling

A look-alike, as the name implies, is a potential customer who looks like a current customer. For example, if your data reveals that your best customers live in California, use Instagram frequently, and are over age 40, you'd be smart to focus your future marketing efforts on people who meet this description. Of course, if you don't capture the data, you'll never know that this is your target audience; normalizing your data gives you this information.

In some instances—in particular for online advertising— you can literally target your advertising to focus only on these high-potential customers. You can even give Google or Facebook the emails of your best customers, and they will figure out the look-alikes for you. In cases where you can't control the targeting as granularly, you can still use this data to your advantage. For example, you could decide to use Instagram as your primary social media channel instead of Facebook or Pinterest, based on the knowledge you have about where your best customers are spending their time.

Audience Suppression

The inverse of look-alike modeling is audience suppression. Suppression means deciding not to engage with a particular set of people. For example, you could exclude people from countries or states where no one seems to want to buy your product, or you could even choose to suppress existing customers who are unlikely to or can't buy your product (if someone bought a new car yesterday, they probably aren't going to buy another one tomorrow).

This ultimately saves you time and money because you are eliminating people who will not drive profit (and as a result, your competitors who aren't doing this will probably end up wasting their time and money on these low-quality prospects).

Personalization

As you capture data on how people are interacting with your business, you can start to customize each person's interaction with your brand and site. This can include changing the offers you present to them (if you know someone is looking to travel to Thailand, you can send them an email with a Thailand travel offer), offering different levels of customer service, encouraging customers to repurchase on a regular basis, and so on.

Segmentation

If you don't have enough data to create personalized messages, you can still differentiate your messages based on broad trends you see across different groups of people. This is known as segmentation. For example, if people in California are interested in buying sunscreen and people in Minnesota are looking for winter coats, it makes sense to send these different audience segments different offers.

Lifetime Value (LTV) Modeling

LTV stands for lifetime value and basically means the total amount of money you make from a particular customer. For example, if you have a customer who spends $10 a month with you for one year and then leaves, the LTV is $120 ($10 times 12 months). For many businesses, the LTV varies dramatically across their customer base. The most loyal customers might make large purchases daily, while another group of customers purchase a small amount once or twice and never come back.

LTV data can therefore be used for segmentation, look-alike modeling, and audience suppression. If, for example, you discover that the LTV of people who found you from Google is $500 and the LTV of people who found you from Facebook is $200, you can spend more money acquiring customers on Google than on Facebook. Of course, if you can figure out LTV at a more granular level (people who bought on Google from California versus Alaska), you can get even better results.

Next, the primary use cases of attribution include the following.

Bid Management

Pretty much any online advertising platform uses auction-based bidding to determine which advertiser shows up on a given placement (for example, when you search for "blue widgets" on Google, the first result you see is basically the advertiser who bid the most to show up there).

Understanding the true value of a given advertising placement allows you to make a better bid. Perhaps the keyword "blue widget" looks like it is driving $10 of revenue for every conversion when you look at the Google Ads data, but when you look at it with your attribution software, it is actually only worth $10 because a lot of people who end up converting off your Google Ad previously clicked on a Facebook ad. This 50 percent difference in value would obviously change your maximum bid for this placement significantly.

Media Mix Modeling

Media mix modeling is the art and science of allocating marketing budget across different advertising channels. Whereas bid management is about making decisions at a very granular level, media mix modeling is about making decisions at a more general level. For example, if you have a monthly budget of $10,000 for your advertising, a media mix model would help you figure out where to spend that $10,000 to get maximum return (it might suggest spending $6,000 on Google, $1,000 on direct mail and the rest on PR, for example).

Budget Planning

Should your marketing budget be $10,000 a month or $100,000? Attribution helps you figure out your diminishing marginal returns. In other words, at what point does the next dollar of marketing investment stop making you a profit?

UNFAIR DATA ADVANTAGE #4: MAKING DATA ACTIONABLE

Edward Tufte, a well-known expert on information design,

created a famous and tragic case study on the space shuttle *Challenger* disaster. In the case study, he showed how the NASA scientists had concluded—prior to the launch of the shuttle—that there was a high chance that a launch in cold temperatures would lead to a catastrophic explosion. Sadly, the engineers did a very poor job of clearly presenting this data to the higher-ups at NASA, such that the higher-ups failed to understand the severity of the risk.[4]

For most businesses, fortunately, poor communication does not have literal life-or-death consequences. Figuratively, however, failing to make your data useful (or actionable) can kill your business. As such, companies that are better at presenting and then acting on their data will find that they have an unfair advantage over their competitors.

Successful data actionability requires three things: analytics, visualization, and execution.

ANALYTICS

Analytics is the science of interpreting data. Typically, this is done by someone who either has a degree in data science or statistics or has received training in how to interpret data. Most commonly, the title of such a person inside a

---

4   Edward Tufte, "PowerPoint Does Rocket Science—and Better Techniques for Technical Reports," Edward Tufte, accessed November 6, 2020, https://www.edwardtufte.com/bboard/q-and-a-fetch-msg?msg_id=0001yB.

company is either analyst or data scientist. Data scientists usually have a combination of statistics and computer science training. Common computer science languages used in data science include R, Python, and SQL (pronounced "sequel"). Business analysts often have less computer science background but have training in business analytics and strategy.

Whether you hire a business analyst or a data scientist, this person's job is to help business owners spot differences in data. This can be the result of questions that the business owners ask or through trying to uncover answers without business guidance. A business owner, for example, might ask, "If I increase the price of my services by 20 percent, how many customers will cancel?" This is a business question that your expert might be able to answer by looking at historical pricing changes and the resulting cancellation rates.

Could the business owner figure this out himself? It depends on a few factors: the size of the data set (the bigger the data set, the harder it is to filter the data without software and still find the right information to interpret), the level of statistical certainty required (most businesspeople do not know how to measure statistical significance, meaning that the business owner's interpretation of the data is usually an educated guess rather than a statistical conclusion), and the amount of time the business owner has to run data analysis.

As a business grows, the balance tilts more and more toward having the analyst/data scientist do most of the analysis and expecting the business owner to ask smart questions and provide feedback on each analysis delivered to improve future analyses.

Put another way, as you think about all the data sources, data sets, and tools I've discussed so far, consider that every time you add complexity to your business in any of these areas, you are more likely to need to hire a data scientist to properly analyze your data. **The two biggest mistakes companies make with their data are: analysis paralysis (doing nothing) and poorly interpreting their data, and both of these mistakes are amplified as your data complexity grows.**

Advanced Analytics: Artificial Intelligence (AI) and Machine Learning (ML)

One of the hottest trends in computer science today is the rise of artificial intelligence (AI) and machine learning (ML). Both of these essentially are advanced computer programs that can be taught to figure out complex problems. For example, a data scientist might provide a computer a data set of 500 recent customers of a company and then ask the computer to predict the characteristics of the next 500 customers. The computer would develop a hypothesis based on the initial data set and then test and refine this over time, eventually creating a very accurate predictor of a new customer.

The advantage of AI/ML is that it can process much larger data sets than what human data scientists could do on their own. The disadvantage of AI/ML is that it is often challenging and expensive to set up. Most companies that invest in AI/ML (at least today) don't end up actually using the systems nearly as much as they expected they would because of the complexity of the setup.

For this reason, I recommend deprioritizing AI/ML initiatives until you have mastered the basics of analytics (and frankly, it can take a lifetime to master the basics). Over time, I expect software companies to develop turnkey AI/ML applications that seamlessly plug into your other data sources, but to date, most AI/ML solutions are designed to be used and implemented by data science professionals.

VISUALIZATION

Visualization means presenting your data in a way that makes it easy to understand. This is typically a combination of reports, graphs, and dashboards.

The most common visualization tool today is business intelligence (BI) software. BI software connects with your data sources (CRM, advertising spend, etc.) and allows non-data scientists to (more or less) effortlessly look at the data from different perspectives. As with the space shuttle example above, it is often hard for non-data scientists to understand raw data. BI increases the chances that business owners will see actionable trends in the data.

The most popular BI tools include Tableau (owned by Salesforce), Domo, Microstrategy, Google Data Studio, IBM Cognos, and Qlik. Most BI tools are geared toward enterprise companies (i.e., they are expensive!). The one exception is Google Data Studio, which, like most Google products, offers a fairly robust free version.

Common BI outputs include:

- **Executive dashboards:** This is a snapshot of the overall health of a company, designed to give C-level leaders a quick summary of the most important metrics. This could include recent sales, financials, traffic (website or retail store), marketing performance, factory output, and so on. With this sort of report, C-level leaders can immediately identify problems and opportunities and cascade next steps down the organization.
- **Sales dashboards:** This is another snapshot designed for the sales team. This might include recent sales, regional sales trends, performance by salesperson, progress toward quota, and pipeline health.
- **Marketing dashboards:** Data might include website

or retail store traffic, marketing return on investment (ROI), marketing channel performance, and marketing qualified leads (MQLs).

- **Graphs and reports:** This includes pretty much anything can be turned into a graph or report. Any of the data described in the previous dashboards could be created as a standalone graph. BI tools give users the ability to create on-the-fly reports by following simple step-by-step guides.

As noted, BI tools are intended to help non-data scientists look at data and find ways to improve business outcomes. Alas, this generally does not mean that you can set up these systems without consultants. Most BI tool vendors make a lot of their money by selling implementation consulting to customers. On top of that, you probably need a data scientist to help you figure out which dashboards and graphs are going to provide you with actionable, statistically significant data. Even Google Data Studio's basic free version probably requires some consulting support to get things set up properly.

EXECUTION

At this point in the chapter, you may feel overwhelmed by the different ways that you can collect, process, measure, and visualize your data. If at first you didn't believe that analysis paralysis was a real thing, you are probably a believer now!

Wayne Gretzky famously quipped, "You miss 100 percent of the shots you don't take." The same is true with data: you can be 100 percent confident that your business will not improve if you do nothing with your data.

Data is never 100 percent complete. Your software will never work perfectly, and your models and analysis will always leave you a little nervous that you missed something or didn't make the right interpretation.

Yet despite all of these valid concerns, the best thing you can do for your business is start using your data. You can start by making low-risk, small decisions that will make barely noticeable impacts on your business. If the results aren't what you expected, go back and tweak your model or double-check your sources and try again. Eventually, you will start to see consistent, business-positive results. As your confidence grows, you can take bigger and bigger risks and drive meaningful growth for your business.

As you build your unfair data advantage, you will be frustrated. That's the bad news. The good news is that your competitors who are trying to do that same thing will be equally frustrated. Even better news is that most of your competitors will get so frustrated that they'll throw up their hands and give up. If you persist, you'll figure things out, and that will give you the upper hand.

Throughout this chapter, I've discussed dozens of tools, techniques, and theories. All of these are worthless without execution. Every year, millions of dieting books are sold in America. My guess is that less than 10 percent of the people who buy a dieting book actually lose weight. It's not because the ideas in the book are bad. It's because dieting is actually pretty hard. As a result, most people like the idea of losing weight much more than the actual work of losing weight. The same is true for data. Creating an unfair data advantage is like losing weight: everyone wants to do it, but only people with persistence will end up being successful.

SUMMARY: THE FOUR UNFAIR DATA ADVANTAGES

Data is incredibly powerful, and companies that understand how to extract value out of their data will always defeat companies that do not. This chapter covered a lot of different ways to use your data to outflank the competition. If you want to send the CEO a summary of the best, most powerful ideas, here are the ideas that are most important:

- **Find your proprietary data:** Your business has data that no other company has. If you are a leader in your industry, you probably also have more data than your competition. Identify all the proprietary data you have or should have, where it is stored, and how it could benefit your business and marketing efforts. You will then be able to use this data to see trends and opportunities that your competition cannot.

- **Measure and track your data:** Data is useless unless you can organize it and analyze it precisely. You can create a huge data advantage by creating tracking systems to record all of your marketing, product, financial, and customer activity. Once the tracking is in place, you can measure every piece of data about your business—from online visits to phone calls to product-level cost and profit. This allows you to make all of that proprietary data actionable, and you can start making decisions that give you an edge on the competition.

- **Connect the dots between different data sources:** Data becomes more powerful when you can combine different data sets. For example, combining your CRM data (sales) with your advertising spend data helps you figure out which ad campaigns are not only driving conversions but are driving conversions with very high revenue. Normalizing data across multiple data sets and then applying attribution to give proportional credit are the two ways to combine data for an unfair advantage.

- **Make the data actionable:** The most powerful way to create an unfair data advantage is to actually start using the data. Business owners often need to see data visualized in reports or dashboards to understand the data. Hiring data scientists (either full time or as consultants) is a good way to turn a lot of raw data into reports that businesspeople can actually act on.

CHAPTER 2

YOUR UNFAIR KNOWLEDGE ADVANTAGE

My 10-year-old son—the same one who is deeply concerned about unfair cupcake sharing at school—has been taking jujitsu classes for two years. This year, an 11-year-old (Josh) joined his class as a new student. The kid is about 20 pounds and six inches taller than all of the 10-year-olds in the class, and he's athletic. Yet, every time he spars (fights) with the 10-year-olds, he gets completely dominated.

The jujitsu coach always warns the kid before he spars about what is going to happen: "Remember Josh, Abigail has been doing this for three years—whatever move you try to make, she's seen it 100 times before and will have a counter!" And sure enough, the 11-year-old continually gets beaten by younger kids who anticipate his every move.

What Josh is learning is something we all intuitively know: knowledge is power. More and more, business success is less about brute strength and more about knowledge. Google isn't a great company because it has a pretty logo. It's great because it hires the smartest, most knowledgeable programmers on earth. The best restaurant in your city is probably great because of an amazing chef who has years of experience (read: knowledge).

HOW KNOWLEDGE SAVES YOU MONEY

At 3Q Digital, we see hundreds of companies' Google accounts every year. A few years ago, we started to see a recurring problem in these Google accounts: we would notice a Google search query (what someone types into Google) that wasn't driving sales for our client, so we'd change the settings in Google to exclude this query.

For example, if you are selling blue widgets and someone types in "free blue widgets" into Google, there's a significant chance that this person is unlikely to actually pay for blue widgets. If that data supports this conclusion, it's the job of the agency to stop running ads on this search query, thus saving the client money.

But here's where things got a little strange. We noticed that when we removed the search query from part of the Google account, Google would start running ads against the search query in other parts of the account. This is a little bit too "inside baseball" to explain in great detail here (if you want to read a comprehensive explanation, check out this whitepaper[5]) but suffice to say, we realized that most advertisers had no idea that this was happening to them. They assumed that if they told Google not to show their ads on a certain search query, that was the end of their ad spend on that query. In fact, because of the way that most advertisers set up their Google accounts, the opposite was happening—the ad was still being shown.

As a result of this discovery, we immediately retrained our entire team with a new way of setting up Google advertising accounts. Overnight, we saw our clients' Google performance skyrocket—in some cases, clients were saving hundreds of thousands of dollars a year.

This discovery and subsequent improvement for our clients was only possible because our team had a granular focus on Google advertising and had access to hundreds of millions of dollars of advertising spend across hundreds of Google advertisers. A generalist marketer or a Google marketer with less experience would have never discovered this problem.

---

5   David Rodnitzky, "An Introduction to Alpha Beta Campaign Structure," 3Q Digital, accessed November 6, 2020. https://3qdigital.com/wp-content/uploads/2013/09/An-Introduction-to-Alpha-Beta-Campaign-Structure.pdf).

And so it goes that the best marketing teams are usually made up of very experienced, expert marketers, and thus every company is on a relentless pursuit for top marketing talent, right?

Well, sometimes. It turns out that a lot of businesses that depend on the star programmers at Google for their search results and the master chefs at their local restaurant for fine food don't apply the same standard when it comes to their marketing. Often because of a lack of understanding of the importance of marketing expertise or a lack of proper measurement of marketing performance, **many marketing teams today aren't staffed with experts.** And as someone smarter than me once said, "If you think an expert is expensive, wait until you see what an amateur will cost you!"

This chapter is about how to staff your marketing team with experts. What experts do you need to be successful? How can you evaluate a marketer's expertise? And when should you hire consultants or outside agencies to supplement your internal marketing expertise? If you get this right, you will have a hugely unfair advantage over your competition. Indeed, even if the competition is bigger, older, and stronger—like a well-trained jujitsu fighter—your experts will run circles around bigger foes all day long.

WHAT IS KNOWLEDGE?

What is knowledge? At one level, knowledge fits into the definition that US Supreme Court Justice Potter Stewart gave when asked to define pornography: "I know it when I see it." When you talk to a marketer, you usually have a pretty good sense of their level of knowledge after a few minutes of conversation. They either answer your questions fully and with confidence, or they dodge and stumble.

To gain an unfair knowledge advantage over the competition, however, you need a more rigorous methodology to assess knowledge. With that in mind, I believe there are five primary ways to assess the knowledge of a marketer.

DEGREES AND CERTIFICATIONS

People who have undergraduate or graduate degrees in marketing are likely to have an understanding of the basics of marketing. Some marketing fields offer certifications that can be obtained through a testing process (for example, you can become certified by Google as an advertising expert if you take an annual test and manage a minimum annual budget with Google). I generally think that degrees and certificates are "nice to haves" but not "must haves" when determining marketing knowledge. There are plenty of people who are true experts who have never stepped foot in a marketing class (and that includes me—I majored in Middle Eastern history).

EXPERIENCE

The longer someone has worked in a given field, the more likely they have "learned on someone else's dime." In other words, people with a lot of experience have knowledge of both what to do and what not to do. When you ask them a question, there's a good chance they've heard it many times before and have an immediate answer. On day one of their employment, they can bring solutions to your business that they've successfully implemented at past companies.

There are two caveats when considering experience: first, make sure that the person's knowledge matches the type of knowledge you are trying to obtain. In other words, a marketing generalist with 20 years of broad experience is unlikely to have valuable knowledge about search engine optimization, a technical, specialized field. Second, look for progressive advancement in responsibility when considering an experienced marketer. A 20-year veteran who hasn't been promoted for 10 years is a potential red flag. Experience is only valuable if that person is continually building a foundation of knowledge, and promotions are a great indicator of increasing knowledge.

SPECIALIZATION

"An expert at everything is an expert at nothing." We live in a world of hyper-specialization. Think about your visits to the doctor. Two hundred years ago, everyone went to their general practitioner for whatever ailed them. Today, we might go to a neurologist who specializes in movement disorders with a subspecialty in Parkinson's disease and a sub-subspecialty in Parkinson's disease caused by environmental toxins.

The marketing world is no different. While it is certainly appropriate for very senior marketers—like a chief marketing officer (CMO)—to have a little knowledge on a lot of things, the people you hire to run your daily marketing need to have specialized expertise in whatever marketing specializations are relevant to your business.

To provide an example of the degree to which you may need experts, consider this: most digital advertising agencies have people who only specialize in Google advertising and other people who only specialize in Facebook advertising. Some agencies have Google experts who only focus on You-Tube, others who only focus on Google Maps, and so on.

THOUGHT LEADERSHIP

Over the course of my career, I've written more than 600 blog posts and articles, as well as spoken at dozens of conferences. Anyone who wants to know whether I'm an expert can type in "David Rodnitzky articles" and find plenty of evidence that demonstrates my expertise. Of course, there are many people who don't want to share their knowledge publicly, and then there are some experts who hire ghost-writers to create all of their content. If, however, you come across someone who has clearly written their own material, this is a great litmus test to determine the true expertise of this person. Even better is someone who has written about your specific business vertical and the specific business challenges you are facing.

MEASURABLE SUCCESS

A lot of marketers can come across as polished and knowledgeable but can't point to any evidence that they've translated their knowledge into profit for a company or themselves. By contrast, the best marketers typically have a resume that quantifiably shows how their marketing efforts grew profitability and market share for their employers.

Even better, great marketers have case studies at the ready that will walk you through a specific challenge that the marketer attacked, replete with raw data, creative examples, and charts. It is far better to see evidence of how the marketer solved a problem than just the what (the results) without evidence. Be mindful, however, of the "causation versus correlation" problem—where a marketer works at a fast-growing company and takes credit for the growth when the actual responsibility for the company success actually rested with market conditions, the product, or other factors unrelated to the marketer's work.

HIRE KNOWLEDGE, NOT FRIENDS

This is just one perspective on how to define marketing knowledge. You can take or ignore anything on this list and create your own custom methodology. Whatever you do, don't wing it. Don't rely excessively on your gut reaction to a person or whether that person happens to be a good conversationalist or likes the same sports team that you do. **One of the biggest mistakes companies make is that they hire people they *like* rather than people they *need*. By the same token, companies typically wait too long to fire people they like and act too soon on firing people they don't like.**

If you want to build an unfair knowledge advantage, you have to be rigorous and relentless at constantly evaluating your marketing staff. Insofar as it's possible, this needs to be an evaluation made objectively, with as little emotion as possible. You'll notice in the list of knowledge qualifiers I introduced, I did not mention cultural fit, personality, or any of the soft skills that many companies value. To be clear, at 3Q Digital, culture is very important—so much so that one of our promises to our team is "We don't work with jerks," which means that we will fire team members or clients if they don't treat others with respect. But cultural fit is ultimately secondary to knowledge.

Many years ago, I had a team member who had a huge attitude problem. He thought he was the smartest guy in the room (which might have actually been the truth), and he let everyone in the company know it. He was nearly impossible to manage.

I sat him down in my office and told him, "Bob (not his real name), I've got good news and bad news. The bad news is you're a jerk. The good news is that you're really smart. I can't teach a dumb person to be smart, but I can teach a jerk to be a nice guy."

Almost immediately, he became one of the nicest and most successful members of my team.

The bottom line is you must always be on the hunt for marketers with superior knowledge. If you are always upleveling your knowledge, you will have an advantage over your foes.

TYPES OF MARKETING KNOWLEDGE

There are hundreds, if not thousands, of areas of specialized marketing expertise. As such, creating a comprehensive list wouldn't provide much value to you (and would be painful to aggregate). Whatever list I created, six months after the publication of the book, an entirely new area of specialization would be invented, making the list obsolete.

So rather than list specific areas of expertise, I'm going to describe categories of marketing knowledge. These categories will help you identify the areas that might be most relevant to your business. Then later in the chapter, I'll give you some tips on how to figure out the right mix of marketing knowledge for your company. You'll notice that many of these categories are "either-or" categories, like traditional marketing is whatever digital marketing is not.

Here are the primary categories of marketing knowledge:

- **Traditional versus digital marketing**
  - **Traditional marketing:** Any marketing that existed before the dawn of the internet and mobile phone is called traditional marketing. This includes billboards, radio, TV, print, and direct mail advertising, PR, yellow pages, local directories, in-store placements, and so on.
  - **Digital marketing:** Also known as internet or online advertising, digital marketing is any type of marketing that uses the internet or mobile devices. This includes SEM, SEO, display advertising, mobile ads, video ads (this can also include streaming TV and video apps) and web design.
- **Brand versus performance marketing**
  - **Brand marketing:** Also known as branding, brand marketing is the art and science of establishing your company name, slogan, and logo as a leader in your industry and preferred choice of customers. Brand marketing typically relies on mass marketing to

reach large numbers of customers, such as through TV or billboards. Brand marketers typically define success by increases in brand recognition and consumer preference as opposed to direct ROI from their marketing campaigns.

○ **Performance marketing:** Also known as growth or direct response marketing, the object of performance marketing is to drive measurable profit for every marketing dollar spent. Performance marketing is set up to drive immediate product purchases or capture leads from interested customers. Unlike branding, there is limited interest in measuring the long-term impact that the advertising has on consumer perceptions.

· **Earned and owned marketing versus paid marketing**

○ **Earned and owned marketing:** Also known as organic marketing, earned and owned marketing is any outbound marketing effort that does not require buying advertising. Examples include PR, marketing collateral, social media posts, your website, and SEO. Earned media refers to press mentions or users sharing your content on social media. Owned media is any content that you create and promote directly, such as a blog post or a social media post. Earned and owned media can be digital or traditional and can be measured by branding or performance metrics.

- **Paid marketing:** Paid marketing is generally advertising or sponsorships. Examples include TV, billboards, trade show booths, Facebook ads, and stadium sponsorships. Paid marketing can be traditional or digital and can be brand or performance marketing.

- **Data:** As you've hopefully gleaned from the last chapter, data is crucial to any modern marketing program. Data experts (typically data scientists) know how to collect, normalize, visualize, and interpret data such that it can lead to actionable decisions for marketers and business owners. Data is important for any of the categories described previously to make better and faster decisions that drive performance and—ultimately—an unfair advantage.

- **Creative:** Creative includes graphical or written work designed to express emotion or convey a sales message. This includes TV commercials, ad text for Google, web design, logo design, billboards, and so on. Creative is important for all marketing.

These categories are not mutually exclusive. There is a lot of overlap in the categories. For example, paid marketing exists in both traditional and digital marketing as well as in branding and performance marketing. Data and creative are vital for pretty much every category of marketing.

WHAT SORT OF MARKETING EXPERTISE DOES MY COMPANY NEED?

There are a lot of marketing experts with boundless amounts of knowledge that will be absolutely worthless to your business. An expert at Google advertising, for example, would be largely irrelevant to a company that sells weapons systems to the five biggest governments in the world (I'm pretty sure that the US Army doesn't do a search for "surface-to-air missiles" as part of its process of selecting a vendor). The key to creating an unfair knowledge advantage is finding an expert whose knowledge is actually useful to your business.

Once you've identified the specific areas of expertise your company needs, you then need to figure out whether you can and should invest in these resources internally or outsource the expertise to a consultant or agency.

The best way to determine your specific need for marketing experts and the right mix of in-house and outsourced experts is to ask four questions.

QUESTION #1: WHO ARE MY CUSTOMERS?

To effectively market your business, you need to understand your customers—where they live, what they like, why they buy from you or a competitor, and how they discover your products and services. If you've created an unfair data advantage (described in Chapter 1), you should have answers or educated guesses for all of these questions.

These answers are vital to figuring out the marketing expertise you need. Does 80 percent of your business come from word of mouth? You probably need to invest in professionals who know branding and PR. Is your target customer in an older demographic? Consider a direct mail or TV professional. Do you see massive differences in sales based on the creatives you run on Facebook? You need to hire an expert at social media creative.

Put another way, **once you understand your data, you understand what makes customers buy from you and can double down in the areas of expertise that drive that purchasing behavior.**

QUESTION #2: IS THIS A CORE COMPETENCY OF MY BUSINESS?

Most companies don't have unlimited budgets to hire every area of marketing expertise needed to run highly effective marketing campaigns. As such, most marketing programs are managed by a combination of internal teams and outside consultants or agencies. Part of your job is to be smart about who you hire and who you contract with outside your business.

To figure out this question, ask yourself whether a particular marketing expertise needs to be a core competency of your business. In other words, is this area of expertise so vital to your success that you need to personally oversee it, or is the knowledge in this area so proprietary that it is too risky to let it be seen outside the company?

Let's say, for example, that 95 percent of your revenue comes from organic search traffic (SEO). The success of your entire marketing program depends on this channel! In this case, it may not make sense to hire an outside consultant who may have four or five other clients that he needs to satisfy in addition to you. You need someone 100 percent dedicated to your SEO campaigns (and frankly, you probably need more than one person, lest your SEO expert walk out the door one day with all of the institutional knowledge about the program). By contrast, if you put out a press release once a month and the result has little impact on the business, you don't need to hire a full-time head of public relations (PR).

The other way of looking at this question is to ask yourself: **is my business marketing-driven or product-driven?** A company that makes fighter jets for the military is product-driven: no amount of cool marketing is going to get the government to buy a poor-quality jet (at least I hope not). A company that sells a commodity like bottled water or a very trendy item like designer jeans is marketing-driven: consumers are heavily influenced by marketing when making a purchase decision.

Marketing-driven companies should have large internal marketing teams and pay top dollar for marketing experts in the areas of marketing that are most impactful for the business. Product-driven companies should minimize marketing team size and find experts outside the company to handle most of the marketing work.

Successful marketing leaders focus on hiring mission-critical experts internally and solving less crucial marketing challenges with outsourced solutions. Success for these leaders is measured by data—like ROI and market share—and not by the number of full-time employees on their payroll.

QUESTION #3: HOW WILL I SPEND MY MARKETING BUDGET?

Let's say that your data analysis reveals that a lot of your customers come from online advertising. You therefore conclude that hiring online marketing experts is the right move. But when you look at the budget you've allocated to online marketing, it is only $20,000 a year (and let's assume that you either don't have additional budget to increase this spend, or there simply aren't enough potential customers surfing online to justify a greater spend).

Given your limited budget, does it make sense to spend $100,000 on a great online marketing expert? In some cases, it does make sense—for example, if that $20,000 of spend drives $10 million in sales, your $100,000 hire will pay for herself many times over. By contrast, if you are a small business and your $20,000 drives $100,000 of revenue (which happens to be the majority of your revenue), it may not make sense to hire an internal expert. It may be possible to hire an outside expert for much less and get similar results.

QUESTION #4: WHAT'S THE ROI OF AN INTERNAL HIRE VERSUS AN AGENCY?

One way to think of this is to try to model the ROI of an internal hire versus an external consultant/agency. The cost of an internal hire is a combination of salary, benefits, fixed costs (like giving them a desk and a computer), and any equity you might give them. An external consultant's cost is only their fees. For example, let's say that you hire a $100,000-per-year online marketing expert. You assume 25 percent additional cost for benefits ($25,000) and $5,000 in fixed costs, and you give them equity that you estimate will be worth $25,000 a year. The total annual cost of that hire is $155,000. Let's assume that you can find an outside consultant who will charge you $7,000 per month to manage your online marketing, for an annual cost of $84,000.

You might conclude that the obvious answer here is to hire the external consultant, since you are saving $71,000 a year, but this is not the end of the analysis. Often, companies believe that an internal hire will drive more value than external help because that hire is 100 percent dedicated to the business, has easier access to other teams in the business, and is more passionate about the company's success (and thus will work harder/longer, etc.). While it is impossible to really quantify this (I'll try to later on), you can try to make an estimate.

Assume, for example, that your internal hire's extra work and passion will drive 100 percent more revenue than your external agency—$200,000 of revenue instead of $100,000. Now the equation looks like this: $200,000 of revenue minus $155,000 of cost equals $45,000 of profit, whereas $100,000 of revenue minus $84,000 of cost equals only $16,000. Thus, in this hypothetical scenario, it would make sense to hire the internal expert, even though the cost is higher than outside help.

Keep in mind, however, that in-house teams have less redundancy than an external agency, increasing the risk that knowledge could walk out the door and leave the company at risk. This risk is also very hard to quantify but needs to be considered.

LEAVE NO DOUBT: HOW TO QUANTIFY YOUR UNFAIR KNOWLEDGE ADVANTAGE

One of the most nefarious psychological maladies that infects marketing leaders is confirmation bias. **Confirmation bias is "a tendency to search for or interpret information in a way that confirms one's preconceptions, leading to statistical errors."[6]**

Here's a common example of how confirmation bias manifests itself in marketing organizations: a company hires a new CMO. The CMO wants to put her stamp on the marketing program and starts to look for things to change. She notices that the company has been working with an advertising agency for several years, with seemingly good results. Her best friend from high school happens to run an agency that offers the same services as the existing agency, so she fires the old agency and replaces them with her friend's agency.

Six months later, performance is down. The new agency blames it on the economy, subpar products the company has released, and low-quality internal marketing team members at the company. In truth, the only thing that has changed is the agency, but the CMO falls victim to confirmation bias: "My decision was the right decision. This new agency is better than the old agency—there must be another

---

6 "Confirmation Bias," *Science Daily*, accessed November 6, 2020, https://www.sciencedaily.com/terms/confirmation_bias.htm.

reason for the decline in our marketing performance." So she fires some internal team members, yells at the product team for creating bad products, and sends articles around the office about how the economy is in trouble. After another six months of bad performance, the CMO is fired.

You might be thinking: what if the CMO was right? What if the marketing performance declined because of everything but the agency change? What if the agency change actually blunted the decline in performance? This theory is plausible, but alas, the CMO made a crucial mistake that ultimately prevented her from selling this theory to her management team—she didn't use data to make or validate her decisions!

In Chapter 1, I emphasized the key role that data plays in giving marketing teams unfair advantages. Yet how often do you see company executives make personnel decisions based on "gut"? **To ensure an unfair knowledge advantage, you have to be relentless about quantifying the effectiveness of your marketing team. Every hiring, firing, or in-house-versus-agency decision you make must be grounded in clear metrics that objectively lead you to the right decision.**

There are three ways to quantify whether you have and are maintaining a knowledge advantage.

QUANTIFYING YOUR KNOWLEDGE ADVANTAGE, PART 1: ESTABLISH KEY PERFORMANCE INDICATORS (KPIS)

KPIs are the top metrics that you evaluate to determine the health of your marketing programs. KPIs typically fall into a few categories:

- **Financial:** This includes marketing's contribution to sales, revenue, or profit. As noted in Chapter 1, with the right tracking and systems, you can often connect your marketing programs directly to financial impact on the company.
- **Traffic:** This includes website visits, store visits, downloads of whitepapers, registration for product demonstrations, trade booth visits, media mentions, samples distributed, and so forth.
- **Output:** This includes deliverables by the marketing team, such as articles written, web pages published, reports created, advertisements created, tests performed, etc.

And each of these KPIs is measured by:

- **Period over period:** How did the KPI improve or decline compared to the prior time period? This is typically year over year, quarter over quarter, or month over month.
- **Against plan:** How did the company or marketing team

do compared to the stated goal for the KPI? For example, if a KPI is $500,000 of revenue from marketing this quarter, was this goal met or not?

- **Against competitive data:** How did the company do compared to competitors? This might include market share, growth, brand preference, industry awards, or any other metric that can be easily determined for the company and its competitors.

KPIs need to be agreed upon by the company leadership, marketing leadership, and any marketing teams that have direct responsibility for the KPI. The KPIs should be SMART, which stands for specific, measurable, achievable, realistic, and timely."[7] Note that there is a difference between "realistic" and "easy"—if you expect your marketing team to be world-class, you need to give them goals that are challenging but achievable (and if anyone on the marketing team is advocating for very easy KPIs, that's a red flag that they might not be world-class).

If you've set up your KPIs properly and your marketing team is consistently hitting the KPIs, that's a very good indication that you have built an unfair knowledge advantage (especially if you are consistently beating KPIs related to your performance against the competition).

---

7 "What is a SMART Goal?" Corporate Finance Institute, accessed November 6, 2020, https://corporatefinanceinstitute.com/resources/knowledge/other/smart-goal/.

By the way, all that work you put in to create your unfair data advantage (remember that chapter a few pages back?) will be very useful in capturing and measuring KPIs. So once you've figured out which KPIs you need to hold your team accountable, go back to your business analyst or data scientist, and ask them to set up a regular report that gives you and your team continuous feedback on your goals.

To be clear, simply achieving KPIs is not always proof of an unfair knowledge advantage. KPIs can be set too low, and success can be falsely attributed to the marketing team (for example, if your company develops a revolutionary new product without rival, it's possible that your growth is entirely due to the product, not marketing). But generally speaking, if you've established good KPIs and your marketing team is hitting them, this is a very good sign.

QUANTIFYING YOUR KNOWLEDGE ADVANTAGE, PART 2: COMMISSION EXTERNAL AUDITS

Imagine you run a TV campaign that costs you $500,000, and you see $700,000 in sales as a result. Should you celebrate or panic? Often, marketing teams live in a bubble, having no idea whether their work is best of class or subpar. A good way to assess your internal expertise is to hire outside experts to come in to audit parts of your marketing.

In an audit, an external consultant or agency with specific

expertise will review your marketing and identify opportunities for improvement, point out where best practices aren't being followed, and suggest a plan for how to transform your marketing into best-of-class performance. Some audits last as little as a couple of weeks, and others take months of in-depth analysis. Prices can range from a few thousand dollars to a million dollars if you hire a large consulting firm.

Audits can feel politically tricky for some organizations. An insecure marketing leader may see the mere suggestion of an outside audit as a vote of no confidence or a threat that he will be fired if the results are poor. This can be mitigated by company leadership by stating the rules of the audit upfront.

For example, if you notify the marketing team that the goal of the audit is to help the team get even better and that the company performs audits across all departments on a regular basis, the fear of the audit being used as a means to fire or demote team members will be reduced.

If, however, after assuaging the marketing leader's concerns, the audit reveals gaping holes in the marketing strategy or execution, you need to differentiate between the promise that the audit was not intended as a way to justify termination and the reality that you may have a subpar marketing leader. Remember: nice team members who are underperformers are incredibly dangerous to your business. **If an audit reveals major problems, you need to either have a high degree of confidence that your leader is the right person to fix the problems, or you need to find a new leader who can solve them.**

I talked earlier about the "causation versus correlation" problem—where, for example, a great product makes the marketing KPIs look amazing, even though the marketing team is average at best. An external audit is one way of ferreting out whether the marketing team is lucky or good.

One other important point about audits: often the external consultant or agency offers not only audits but also management of the area they are auditing. As a result, there is the potential that the external consultant might be overly critical of the internal team's work as a way to convince the company leaders to give them ongoing management of the area in question. This is a legitimate concern (and also explains why in-house teams are often very nervous when they are getting externally audited).

There are three ways to reduce the risk that this will happen: first, you can hire an external auditor who does not do ongoing management of what they audit; second, you can make it very clear upfront to the external consultant that they are being paid for the audit only, and that they would not even be eligible to manage the marketing area if the company decided to switch to an agency or consultant; third, you can ask for references from past consulting projects that did not result in the consultant taking over the business. If the company can't give you any such examples, this is a pretty clear sign that their goal with audits is to turn them into full-time management.

Put another way, **audits are very valuable to assess the true expertise of your team, but audits need to be conducted in a fair, transparent way,** with both the internal team and external agency understanding the objectives and deliverables of the audit.

A CASE STUDY ON AUDITS, EXPERIENCE, AND PAYDAY LOANS IN ANGOLA

A few years ago, the CEO of a fast-growing software company invited me to do an audit of his company's SEM campaigns. The company focused on providing online appointment-setting and HR management tools for small businesses in the United States.

The internal marketing team was resistant to the audit, insisting that they were running a flawless SEM program. With pressure from the CEO, they grudgingly granted me access to the account. What I saw was shocking. The company was buying terms like "payday loans" in Angola and wasting thousands of dollars a month. I wrote back to the CEO and gave him my honest assessment.

"This account is a train wreck," I told him.

A few days later, the head of marketing wrote me a terse response: "We are restructuring the account. Come back in three months, and you'll see a perfect account!"

Three months later, I reached out to the CEO and again got access to the account. Fortunately, the company was no longer targeting the lucrative Angolan payday loan market. Even more amazingly, however, the conversion rate in the account was at 96 percent! In other words, according to the data in the account, 96 out of 100 people who clicked on a search ad were converting into customers. The marketing team was giddy with excitement about the dramatic turnaround they had orchestrated.

This is where the value of experience and expertise became so important. Over the course of my 13 years running an SEM agency, I've personally been involved in hundreds of account audits and reviewed hundreds of accounts managed by my team. As a result, I have a good sense of what sort of conversion rate to expect from SEM campaigns. For example, a company offering consumers a free email newsletter with discounts and coupons (think Groupon or Travelzoo) can see conversion rates as high as 20 percent or more from their campaigns. By contrast, a very expensive enterprise software company that is targeting CTOs at Fortune 500 companies might be lucky to get a 0.5 percent conversion rate on an offer to schedule a demo of their product.

This company, a software as a service (SaaS) company targeting small to medium businesses (SMBs) could expect a conversion rate from 2 percent to maybe 6 or 7 percent. So my experience immediately told me something wasn't right about the data the marketing team was reporting.

Then my expertise kicked in. With my modest understanding of how conversion rate is measured in online marketing, I looked at the source code of the company's landing pages. What I discovered was that the marketing team had placed the conversion pixel (the piece of code that tells Google to report a success conversion event) on the landing page and not on the "thank you" page. Put another way, every person who clicked on an SEM ad was being recorded as a conversion unless they left so quickly that the conversion pixel didn't even have time to fire (this is known as a bounce and is measured as bounce rate). When the team fixed the pixel location, the conversion rate dropped to the single digits.

Without external help from an expert, who knows? Perhaps this company would still be celebrating worthless conversions and donating a lot of money to Google in the process. Unfortunately, for many companies, such marketing malpractice might actually bankrupt the company.

QUANTIFYING YOUR KNOWLEDGE ADVANTAGE, PART 3: ALWAYS BE TESTING

A friend of mine wrote a book about user testing for web pages. He recounted his experience working with companies to improve the usability of their websites. Often, he noted, the CEO or CMO would have an opinion about what was going to work best on their site (this is sarcastically referred to as HIPPO—the highest paid person's opinion). My friend always has the same retort when he gets these ideas from C-level executives, and it's the name of his book: *You Should Test That!* In other words, opinions don't matter; data matters!

As the CEO of an agency, one of the most frustrating experiences I had to deal with regularly was the CMO who said, "We are a data-driven company—we test everything," and then proceeded to either hire a new agency or replace his existing agency with an in-house team without any data-driven process or reasoning.

Many years ago, we had a client for whom we drove an extra $50 million in sales in less than six months. The CEO then called me up and told us we were fired. His reason: he needed a "forcing function" to help his in-house team learn online marketing as quickly as possible. His assumption was that an in-house team would quickly surpass the performance of the agency. Maybe he was right, but is it worth $50 million to follow your gut?

If you really want to create a knowledge advantage, you have to be agnostic about where that knowledge sits and use data to figure out the answer. Thinking about switching agencies? Set up a test that allows the incumbent agency to compete against the new agency. Unsure that one of your marketing experts is at the top of his game? Set up a test to see how the campaigns he manages perform against campaigns managed by someone else.

To be clear, setting up a perfectly objective test is challenging if not impossible. Marketing is not like a 100-meter dash, where you can measure competitors within a hundredth of a second. But remember the adage: **don't let the perfect get in the way of the good.** Even if your test is directional, you can still use the results to assess and potentially uplevel your unfair marketing advantage.

Here are a few common ways that companies test their marketing knowledge:

- **Geographic split test**: Give your existing team or agency one geographic area, and give the challenger a similarly situated but different geographic area. For example, one agency gets the Western United States, and one agency gets the Eastern United States. Each runs campaigns for 60 days, and then you award the business to the team that drove the best results. This is easy to do for paid advertising (like Google campaigns), where the user interface is designed to allow for geographic targeting. For areas like PR and earned social media, it can be harder to find a natural geographic breakdown to test.

- **Break the account in half (by product, business unit, etc.):** Sometimes accounts are more easily tested at product- or business-line level. For example, if a company has a toothpaste brand and a mouthwash brand, you could give one brand to one team and one to another.

- **Consumer surveys:** Sometimes a company doesn't want to run a public test to get results, so the geographic or product split tests won't work. For example, if you are testing out a new brand agency that has suggested a very different branding slogan and focus for your business, running this campaign "in the wild" to millions of customers can have a negative impact on your business (if the brand turns off consumers). So an alternative approach is to do a survey or poll of a smaller group of customers to get feedback. In the brand world, this might mean showing consumers two different brand concepts and surveying them to determine whether their perception of and preference for the brand increased or declined as a result of the new messaging.

SUMMARIZING THE KNOWLEDGE ADVANTAGE

I started this chapter by observing that knowledge is difficult to define. This is a blessing and a curse. It's a curse in the sense that it is hard to really know with 100 percent certainty that you have a knowledge advantage. It's a blessing because the difficulty in measuring knowledge results in most companies failing when it comes to assessing their marketing knowledge. Add to this the reality that most companies keep really nice but average employees, and you have a significant opportunity to outflank the competition with superior knowledge.

If you can develop systems to constantly measure and uplevel your marketing knowledge—and if you can remain impartial about the data—you will create a massive unfair advantage for your business. To make this happen, you need to:

- Use data to identify the marketing knowledge that is vital for your business success.
- Hire experts who have demonstrated knowledge in these specific marketing competencies.
- Understand when to invest in internal expertise and when to outsource.
- Establish SMART KPIs that enable you to track the actual performance of your experts.
- Constantly challenge your assumptions by coming up with metrics-driven tests to evaluate the knowledge of your experts.

CHAPTER 3

YOUR UNFAIR ACCESS ADVANTAGE

A few years ago, my brother got an internship with a venture capital firm in Silicon Valley. While at that firm, he met another venture capitalist who happened to work in the same building. He introduced me to that venture capitalist, who then introduced me to the founders of a small company that he had invested in. The founders of that company introduced me to their new CEO, and the new CEO introduced me to a friend of his working at another startup. That startup friend introduced me to another venture capitalist, who introduced me to the CEO of another startup that became a client of 3Q (and subsequently has resulted in several additional clients as members of the marketing team left for new opportunities).

This sort of "friend of a friend of a friend" connection game is common in Silicon Valley. I often say that Silicon Valley is a small valley—your reputation is everything here, and people and companies that do good work grow their businesses quickly, while those that don't end up leaving with their tail between their legs.

But there's another important takeaway from this business networking: living and working in Silicon Valley has given me—and my agency, 3Q Digital—an unfair access advantage. Our physical location in this area has enabled us to meet the founders of many well-funded companies and the venture capitalists at many prominent venture capital firms. As a result, many of these companies often chose to work with 3Q Digital without even talking to our competitors. A recommendation from a trusted investor or fellow entrepreneur was enough to convince them that we were the right agency for them.

An agency in Florida or Michigan will have a much more difficult time building connections in Silicon Valley and—unless they are constantly traveling here—will have more superficial relationships, since they can't have the on-the-fly in-person meetings we have. By contrast, if 3Q Digital wanted to win a lot of oil and gas clients, we'd be at a disadvantage to an agency based in Texas or Alberta for the same reason.

Every business has access advantages like the one described, yet many marketing teams fail to use these advantages to benefit their company's marketing program.

THE FOUR UNFAIR ACCESS ADVANTAGES FOR MARKETING

Your business, and specifically your marketing team, has clout and connections that your competitors don't. If you are the biggest advertiser in your local newspaper, you will get special privileges and opportunities that an average advertiser will not. If you happen to have gone to college with a writer from *The New York Times* who covers your industry, you are far more likely to get this writer to discuss your business than your competitor who has no connection to her.

Here are four ways you can use your unfair access to benefit your marketing programs.

ACCESS ADVANTAGE #1: ACCESS TO AUDIENCES

There are thousands of different places to advertise your products. I discussed broad categories of advertising in the last chapter (traditional versus online, performance versus branding). Within each of these categories are individual publishers (I am using the term "publisher" broadly to include any place where you can buy an advertisement, not just a print publication), each of which has a sales team ready to sell you an advertisement.

This is an opportunity and a problem. It's an opportunity because there are so many different places to advertise, and if one publisher doesn't drive the results you want, you can test another. It's a problem because there are simply too many publishers for any one advertiser to test. Moreover, some of the largest publishers restrict who they let advertise with them. While this sounds crazy (isn't all money equally green?), large publishers actually have two good reasons to limit their list of advertisers.

The first reason is time. Publishers only have so many sales reps, so they can't field calls from every advertiser in the world. They have to manage their time to ensure that the most profitable advertisers get served first, which usually means that they don't have time for many potential advertisers.

The second reason is money. Setting up an advertisement can often be very expensive (imagine creating a billboard near a highway—getting a billboard live requires design, large-format printing, and a crew to actually paste up the billboard on the side of the road). If a sales team sells too small of a contract, the work required to fulfill the order might cost more than the revenue that the publisher gets from the advertising.

As a result of these two constraints, there is a lot of advertising inventory in the world that is off-limits to most advertisers! Put another way, **there is a small set of advertisers who have an unfair access advantage to large chunks of advertising placements.**

Now think of your marketing team and consider these two barriers. First, do you have relationships with publisher sales teams that your competitors don't? Perhaps you started working with the publisher when they were smaller and more open to working with companies of your size. Or perhaps you know someone on the publisher sales team from a past position where they did business with your marketing team. However the relationship was formed, if you have a sales team that will talk to you and not to the competition, you have an opportunity to buy ads that your competitor can't.

The same exercise applies to your advertising budgets. Perhaps you don't have the budget to buy a $5 million Super Bowl ad, but you can invest enough to buy three or four billboards around your hometown. Your ability to buy at scale at a local level may open up advertising inventory to you that your competitors can't afford.

One other important point about access to advertising: the buying and selling of advertising is often a highly inefficient process. Take billboards as an example. If a local billboard company has 50 billboards that they can sell for the month of June, the sales team will work hard to sell out all the inventory prior to the beginning of the month. Often, however, the sales team is not 100 percent successful, and a few days before the start of the month, there are some billboards that haven't been sold.

These billboards are fungible; like fruit at the supermarket, if they aren't sold by a certain date, they become worthless. Supermarkets and advertising sales teams approach this problem in the same way. The closer they get to the date that the product loses its value, the more creative they get at trying to sell the product. At the supermarket, fruit that is getting close to rotting is put on sale at a deep discount. The same happens with advertising. A June billboard slot that might have been for sale for $10,000 in early May might be available for $2,500 on the last day of the month (this is known as remnant inventory).

This is where access can be an incredible unfair marketing advantage because advertising sales teams are going to call the advertisers they know to unload this inventory. So **not only does access allow you to run ads where your competitors can't, but it sometimes enables you to run these ads at clearance prices,** thus increasing the ROI of the ad.

HOW TO ESTABLISH YOURSELF AS A LEGITIMATE BUYER OF REMNANT INVENTORY

To effectively buy remnant media, you have to be ready to move quickly. After all, this is usually inventory that will disappear into thin air if it isn't immediately sold by the sales team. To establish yourself as the "go to" marketer with any sales team, take the following steps:

- **Be clear with publishers about the type of remnant you want to buy.** Let salespeople know what types of opportunities are most interesting to you, including price, type of ad, time range, and so on. Continue to reach out to them and remind them that you are ready to buy media that fits these criteria.
- **Get preapproved internally to make remnant media buys.** With time of the essence, you don't have the luxury of running a remnant media buy through a few weeks of internal approvals (the opportunity will have come and gone). So you need preapproval. For example, your CEO or CMO might authorize a media buy of up to $25,000 per week that you can sign without any additional review.
- **Be ready to wire money ASAP.** Unless you have established a line of credit with the media publisher, you need to be ready to pay for the media buy on a moment's notice. This means working with your finance team to ensure that there's a process in place (and money in the bank) to quickly wire

money to the publisher, often within a few hours of contract signature.

- **Have creative ready to go**. Understand the creative requirements of each publisher—what size the ad should be, what is and isn't permitted, who you should send it to, and what sort of tracking is needed or allowed. For publishers with which you are repeatedly buying last-minute placements, send them creative you've preapproved to run in the event your creative team can't get them new creative in time.

Note that the advertising world is changing, in that more and more advertising inventory is being sold programmatically—by computerized systems—instead of through one-to-one connections between sales teams and media buyers. Most digital advertising is sold programmatically, which significantly reduces the access advantage for marketing teams (there are other access advantages that apply to digital advertising, which I'll discuss later).

ACCESS ADVANTAGE #2: ACCESS TO TESTING

I recently got a call from one of 3Q Digital's account managers at a very large digital publisher. The account manager told me that his company had a new optimization algorithm that they were testing. He said that the internal results showed that the algorithm should significantly improve ROI for advertisers but that they hadn't tested it with any actual advertisers. As such, he "made me an offer I couldn't refuse"—let him run this algorithm on a few 3Q Digital clients to assess the results. If at any point the algorithm cost the clients money, his company would reimburse the clients 100 percent.

This is a win-win for our clients. First, they get access to technology that is believed to be superior to the existing systems. Assuming the tech works as planned, this means that the clients are getting better results than their competitors who have no ability to use the same technology. Second, if the technology doesn't work, there's no risk to them (and actually, the "failed" tech can still end up being a benefit to the client because all of the unprofitable impressions and clicks that the clients get are free branding).

It is very common for digital publishers to run tests like these. These are sometimes called alphas (which usually means an internal test that has not been publicly announced with a very small set of external testers—usually only the biggest agencies and advertisers get access to these) or betas (a publicly announced test with a larger set of testers). The more connections an advertiser has with the publisher—and often the more money the advertiser is spending—the more likely it is that they will be offered participation in the test.

Of course, this is not just limited to advertising. If you are a large user of a marketing software solution or you spend a lot of money with a service provider like a consulting firm, you will have opportunities to get in early on tests, often for free or at cost to the service provider.

ACCESS ADVANTAGE #3: ACCESS TO INFLUENCE

A few years ago, I wrote an article about getting blacklisted on Google. Google has a long list of rules that advertisers have to follow to be allowed to run ads on the search engine. If an advertiser violates a rule, Google has a policy team that can decide to kick the advertiser off Google—forever. This can be financially disastrous for the advertiser. For many advertisers, Google represents more than 50 percent of their sales, and getting banned would almost certainly lead to the closure of their business.

In my article, I talked about different techniques my agency had used to help companies get back onto Google, even after being blacklisted. As a result of the article, a company emailed me asking for help. They had recently been blacklisted because a junior employee hadn't read Google's rules and had posted an ad with images that clearly violated Google's terms. The company had tried to reach out to Google numerous times but couldn't get any further than terse emails from an anonymous customer service representative. So the company asked if 3Q Digital could help.

I reviewed the violation that the company had committed and concluded that it was a genuine mistake and that the company had a history of working hard to comply with Google's rules. I then created a PowerPoint presentation that outlined all the reasons I felt that the company had been unfairly banned from Google and sent it to an account manager at Google. I also let Google know that if the account was reapproved, 3Q Digital would manage the campaigns going forward, and that our reputation for being a good partner that follows the rules should also factor into their decision. The account manager forwarded it to the policy team, which agreed to reinstate the advertiser. I should note that seven years later, the advertiser is now profitably spending almost $10 million a year with Google!

This is an example of how access can create influence that gives you an unfair advantage. In this instance, it was using influence to overturn a policy decision, but there are many other ways that influence can work in your favor. Influence can help shape product decisions with your marketing partners. If you depend on marketing software but the software is lacking a feature that would really accelerate your business, you can push the provider to either build a custom solution for you or prioritize this feature in their next product release.

Influence can also drive direct revenue for your business. A few years ago, a prominent entrepreneur was struggling with her Google advertising campaigns. She reached out to a few senior people at Google for agency recommendations. Google came back to her with a list of 10 agencies. One of the senior people at Google said, "We can't recommend one agency over another, but you should call the agency at the top of the list." A week later, we got a call from the entrepreneur and signed her as a client. Relatedly, if you believe that you are entitled to a refund or a credit from a marketing partner, having influence inside that company will give you a better chance of getting someone on the finance team to agree with your demand.

ACCESS ADVANTAGE #4: ACCESS TO PUBLICITY

When Jay-Z launched Tidal, his online music streaming service, he didn't just send out a press release and hope that someone wrote about it. Instead, he hosted a launch event with a few of his friends, which included Usher, Rihanna, Nicki Minaj, Madonna, Deadmau5, Kanye West, Jason Aldean, Jack White, Daft Punk, Beyonce, and Win Butler. As you can see from the interest on Google, the event got a lot of attention.[8]

---

8   "tidal," Google Trends, accessed April 7, 2021, https://trends.google.com/trends/explore?date=2015-01-01%202021-04-07&q=tidal&hl=en-US.

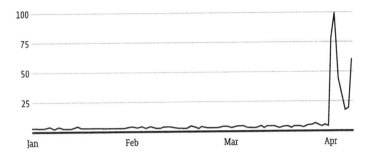

Interest over Time

If you or I wanted to have Madonna attend the launch party of our business, it would probably cost us a couple million dollars (and even then, I'm not sure she'd attend). But amazingly, Madonna actually paid to attend this event (she and the other stars were convinced by Jay-Z to invest in his music service and then attend the launch for free).

You don't need to be Jay-Z to get unfair access to publicity. Firstly, everyone is connected to someone who can bring publicity to your business. You may have a cousin who played in the NFL, or your neighbor may be the mayor of your city, or a classmate from college may be writing for a major newspaper. **We all know people who are in some shape or form influential, and if you can leverage these people to help your business, you will drive free publicity.**

Obviously, you don't want to ruin your relationships by crassly demanding that your connections shill for your business. But your access to these people at least enables you to start the conversation. Again, think of Madonna—what are the chances that you could even get an email back from her publicist? Probably very slim. So whatever ideas you have around getting Madonna to endorse your business will likely never come to fruition. If your competitor, however, happened to have gone to grade school with Madonna's brother, that may be just the connection she needs to get that initial email back from someone on Madonna's team that might eventually lead to some sort of business relationship—that is an unfair access advantage!

Second, you may be a celebrity yourself! It may feel uncomfortable to label yourself as such, but celebrity status is not just limited to Hollywood A-listers and world leaders. Being a recognized leader in your industry is a great way to get free publicity for your business. And becoming a leader is often not as hard as you think.

In my case, back in 2004, I was frustrated by the quality of writing I saw in articles about search engine marketing. So I started a personal blog to share my opinions and strategies. In the early days of this blog, I had two readers—my mom and dad! But I kept writing the blog, and slowly I noticed that I was getting more comments and more subscribers. After a couple of years, I started applying to speak at industry conferences. Once I did one or two, I became a member of the speaker circuit (the group of people you see at every industry conference). This becomes a self-fulfilling prophecy—once you are on the circuit, you are almost assured of getting accepted to the next conference because you are now considered a leader.

LEAVE THEM SCRATCHING THEIR HEADS

Whenever I present at a conference, my mantra is simple: I want the audience to leave scratching their heads instead of yawning. Put another way: **I never simplify my presentations to pander to beginners in the crowd. I want even the most advanced marketers to leave my talk with their heads full of advanced and new information.**

I've been on numerous panels where I've given the audience advanced, often proprietary knowledge and my fellow panelists have offered watered-down, marketing 101 platitudes. After the panel is finished, the line of people who want to talk to the other panelists is often longer than the line to talk to me. And while it's possible that I'm just not that dynamic of a speaker, my observation is that the quality of conversations and seniority of the people I interact with after the panel are significantly higher than those of my peers, who spend their time re-explaining marketing basics to the newbies in the crowd.

Put another way, if you had the choice of talking to 10 junior marketers or one CMO, which conversation would be the most likely to drive a better outcome for your business? For me, I'll take talking to the CMO every time. This is not to say that I don't enjoy training and mentoring young marketers. From an ROI for my business perspective, however, using my unfair knowledge advantage to access CMOs is the right choice.

The same thinking applies to conversations with journalists. Journalists are assigned a beat or specific area that they need to report on. As a result, they become very knowledgeable of the beat and can process a lot of sophisticated information. I'd much rather have a detailed, expert-level conversation with a journalist than a high-level overview discussion. Top journalists gravitate to true experts.

As a result of the speaking gigs, I started getting contacted by journalists, and I appeared in news stories. I also started to submit guest articles to larger publications (like *Entrepreneur* magazine and *Huffington Post*) that were accepted because I had built up a reputation as an expert.

All of this is a roundabout way of pointing out that you don't need to be born famous to become famous, at least in your niche. Once you've built up your reputation, you can leverage it to get tons of free publicity, which drives business!

SUMMARIZING THE ACCESS ADVANTAGE

Access feels like the ultimate unfair advantage. It really stings your competition when your marketing outperforms them because of who you know and have access to! As noted, we all have an access advantage—whether it is to a prominent figure, ad inventory available to the select few, opportunities to test products and services before they are available to the general public, or free publicity. You should assume that your competitors are actively identifying their unfair access advantages. After all, they are all probably reading this book too. Find your access advantage to level the playing field!

CHAPTER 4

YOUR UNFAIR BRAND ADVANTAGE

There's a famous expression about business that states: "No one ever got fired for choosing IBM." IBM is a giant, well-regarded company. As such, the argument goes, it's safer to choose an IBM product over a smaller competitor's product. After all, if the IBM product fails, the buyer can say, "Don't blame me; I chose IBM." The TLA (three-letter acronym) for this sort of decision-making is FUD—fear, uncertainty, and doubt. Big, established companies use FUD all the time to convince buyers that their decision should be based on career safety, not on product quality, price, or other factors that you'd generally think are pretty important.

Put another way, IBM's brand is an unfair marketing advantage. Smaller companies with better service, price, product—whatever—may lose against IBM for no other reason than the power of IBM's brand!

Building a brand is neither easy nor cheap. Most big brands have spent years and a lot of money to establish their specific brand identity. This chapter has no shortcuts to help you create a brand out of thin air. What this chapter is about is leveraging your brand across all of your marketing. Many marketers take a narrow view of the role of branding in marketing and thus fail to exploit their brand's true power. This chapter helps you think creatively about how to extend your unfair brand advantage.

WHAT IS BRANDING?

When I did a search on Google for the definition of branding, the first definition I got was "the action of marking with a branding iron." While this is the origin of the term (farmers marking their livestock with their initials or a unique shape in case they get lost), the definition I'll use for this chapter is from *Entrepreneur*: "Your brand is your promise to your customer. It tells them what they can expect from your products and services, and it differentiates your offering from that of your competitors."[9] Like the original branding definition, you definitely don't want your brand to get lost, and you want people to find it.

9   "Branding," *Entrepreneur*, accessed November 6, 2020, https://www.entrepreneur.com/encyclopedia/branding.

If your brand sets the expectation for customers (the promise), branding is the art and science of spreading and reinforcing this expectation to as many customers as possible. Brand marketers focus on messaging, logos, slogans, advertising, and emotional experiences that are all intended to ensure that when a potential customer is considering a purchase in their category of products or services, the customer clearly understands why they should (or should not) buy the marketer's product.

Sometimes the branding is designed to evoke exclusivity and luxury (Rolex, Mercedes, Four Seasons Hotels); sometimes it is fun (Carnival Cruises, Disney, Dave and Busters), safety (Volvo), intelligence (McKinsey Consulting), and so on.

Unlike direct marketers—who are focused on driving measurable profit from their marketing efforts—brand marketers focus on long-term, less directly measurable metrics. Three of the most common metrics of branding are awareness (have potential customers heard of the brand?), preference (do potential customers indicate a preference for one brand over another?), and lift (is the number of potential customers who have awareness and preference for a brand increasing?). Much of this can be measured through customer surveys, but it is also possible to look for trends in direct type-ins of a brand name into an internet browser, searches for the brand, and correlated increases in store traffic and overall sales.

Once a brand has been successfully established, there are many obvious and positive impacts on the underlying business. These include:

- **Increased prices:** Customers will pay more money for a brand they trust versus an unknown brand.
- **Free publicity:** Leading brands get a lot of free news coverage. If a journalist is writing an article on soda, for example, you can be sure that the journalist will reference Coke and Pepsi in the article.
- **Brand extension:** Companies can expand into new categories of services or products by leveraging the brand reputation of their existing products. Virgin, for example, established a brand as a "hip" record company and successfully extended this brand to airlines, stores, trains, and a cruise line.
- **Decreased reliance on advertising:** Successful branding programs can create enough product preference and awareness with potential customers that the brand becomes the de facto choice in the category. The most successful brands can actually transition from nouns to verbs! For example, "I don't know the answer to that question. I'll Google it." Or, "Let's not drive tonight. Let's Uber." And the most recent brand to make that transition, "Let's Zoom to talk about it!" For these particularly successful brands, it is possible to reduce advertising budgets and let the brand carry the company forward.

These are all objectives that brand marketers hope and plan for, and this chapter won't discuss them in too much detail. There are thousands of books that have described the power of branding.

Instead, this chapter is about the less obvious ways to use your brand for an unfair advantage. I've uncovered four hidden and unfair brand advantages that will directly benefit your marketing.

UNFAIR BRAND ADVANTAGE #1: IMPROVED DIRECT RESPONSE

Earlier in this chapter, I mentioned that really effective branding can help you reduce your direct response advertising budget. Even the most successful brands, however, typically continue to use direct response advertising as part of their marketing strategy. Companies like Google and Uber, for example, spend more than $100 million a year on direct response advertising, despite their success at branding.

What many companies don't realize is that their brand—used properly—can have a dramatic and positive impact on their direct response advertising. The best way to understand how this can happen is to go back to the KPIs that direct response advertisers value: profit metrics like ROI and Return on Advertising Spend (ROAS) and efficiency metrics like Cost Per Action (CPA) and Cost Per Install (CPI).

Imagine that two companies each send 1,000 direct mail postcards to the same set of potential customers. GEICO is a well-publicized and respected insurance brand; the other company, "Lizard Insurance," is a newly launched startup. Each marketing team evaluates their performance at the end of the campaign, and they see the following:

GEICO:

- 25 responses (2.5 percent)
- 5 purchases (25 percent from response to purchase)
- $1,000 average order value (5 × $1,000 = $5,000)
- Cost of campaign: $2,500
- Profit of campaign: $2,500

Lizard:

- 20 responses (2 percent)
- 3 purchases (15 percent from response to purchase)
- $800 average order value (3 × $800 = $2,400)
- Cost of campaign: $2,500
- Profit of campaign: -$100

As you can see from this example, the GEICO campaign drove more than double the revenue of the startup campaign. GEICO drove $2,500 of profit, while the startup lost $100. Since direct response marketers are charged with driving profit from their advertising campaigns, the likely result of these two outcomes is a doubling down of direct mail advertising by the brand and a cessation of these campaigns by the startup.

In other words, an entire channel of direct response advertising could be available to the brand and not to the startup simply because the brand has the unfair advantage of their brand recognition, which drives more conversions and higher purchase amounts.

This brand advantage is even more evident in the world of online advertising, like Google and Facebook. Google and Facebook run real-time auctions to determine which advertisers show up in a consumer's search results or on their news feed on the social network.

Unlike an auction on eBay, however, the winning bids on online advertising auctions are not solely determined by who is willing to make the highest bid. Instead, the auction is determined by a combination of the highest bid or cost per click (CPC) and the highest click-through rate (CTR). This is designed to simultaneously make money for the advertising platform and ensure that the ads are relevant to consumers. So, if Advertiser A bids $5 per click and has a 10 percent CTR but Advertiser B is willing to pay $1 per click and has a 70 percent CTR, Advertiser B would win the auction.

Google basically optimizes to maximize their revenue per thousand impressions (RPM). If you do the math, you can see how this benefits Google and Facebook:

- $5 per click with 10 percent CTR results in 100 clicks and $500 of revenue for every 1,000 impressions ($500 RPM).
- $1 per click with 70 percent CTR results in 700 clicks and $700 of revenue for every 1,000 impressions ($700 RPM).

This is a double whammy of unfair advantage for brands. First, as shown in the direct mail example, brands typically get better consumer response. In the case of online advertising, this means that more customers are likely to click on an advertisement from a brand they recognize than from an unknown brand. The higher the CTR, the lower the advertiser has to pay to show up at the top of the ad results. So it **may be the case that a brand is paying $1 per click and a startup is paying $5 for that same click simply because of the power of the brand to drive high CTR.**

Second, the brand is likely to have a higher conversion rate on their offer. FUD drives customers to choose an established brand much of the time. So not only do the brands pay less per click; they may be getting more sales and revenue per click.

Suffice to say, if you have built a brand for your business, you need to leverage that brand in your direct response marketing. This manifests itself in a few ways:

- **Mention your brand name and your brand tagline/slogan frequently.** If you are allowed to use graphics, show your logo or mascot in all of your creative.
- **Use FUD!** For example, if you are an established bank competing against online banks that offer better service or interest rates, consider an ad that says, "Brand Name Bank. Trusted by One Million Customers Since 1905. FDIC Insured."
- **Defend your turf.** Google, for example, allows advertisers to bid on the brand keywords of competitors. Some brands refuse to bid on their brand terms and instead hope that customers will ignore the paid ads of competitors and go directly to the brand's organic (free) listings. In many instances, this is a mistake. We have done numerous studies for our clients that show that buying your own brand terms is a net positive for your business. This is done through the concept of an incrementality study, which I discussed in the analytics section.

UNFAIR BRAND ADVANTAGE #2: PEOPLE WILL ANSWER YOUR CALLS

Most experienced business professionals are inundated with unsolicited calls, emails, texts, and letters from people trying to sell them something. I have seen salespeople go to great lengths to get my attention. One company sent a guy dressed as a chef to my office and dropped off an apple pie with a custom message on the pie about why I should work with them. Another delivered a four-foot-long helicopter with a note attached to it that said, "If you want the remote control for this helicopter, let me meet with you in person for 30 minutes" (it worked!).

The vast majority of these outreach attempts, however, end up being deleted or trashed, often without any serious consideration of the offer. An outreach from an established brand, however, is far more likely to get a response. I (half-jokingly) tell people that I would never hire a salesperson from Google. Why? Because pretty much anyone who gets a call from someone at Google is going to take the call. Google is one of the most valuable brands in the world. Who wouldn't want to hear from a Google salesperson? It's like selling water in the Sahara.

Recall that I discussed access to advertising as an unfair access advantage in the last chapter. If you work for an established brand, you have that same access advantage, even if you don't know a single person at the publisher.

Salespeople have limited time and need to focus their pitches on the advertisers most likely to spend a lot of money with their company. **A call from the marketing team at Pepsi is going to get returned a lot quicker than a call from an unknown brand.** Moreover, a publisher might let Pepsi do a $10,000 test with them in the hopes that this test leads to a much larger spend. However, they would be reluctant to do the same with a non-brand simply because they have lower expectations of increased future spend.

The same is true with publicity. **Brands get a lot of free press when journalists reach out to them for a quote in a story, but brands also have a lot more success at pitching stories to journalists.** If a local coffee company decided to offer their baristas tuition assistance as a perk, it's unlikely that the *New York Times* would cover the news. But do a search for "Starbucks tuition" on Google News, and you'll find more than 22,000 stories! Brands can literally create positive news about themselves and further enhance their brand value.

Remember, your brand doesn't have to be Nike or Coke to gain an unfair advantage. If you are the biggest car dealer in your small city or the top immigration law firm, you have a brand within your unique sphere of influence that will get important people to call you back and want to do business with you.

One (hopefully obvious) caveat: brands work because they reinforce an expectation or promise. When a brand doesn't deliver on that promise, the brand can be permanently damaged. As such, whenever you use your brand to gain unfair access, you have to make sure that you deliver on the expectation you are setting with the partner.

For example, if Pepsi called up 100 newspapers and said, "We are making a huge announcement next week; we need you at headquarters," a good number of those news outlets would send reporters to the event. If, at the event, Pepsi failed to announce anything significant, the brand of the Pepsi marketing team would be damaged. The next time Pepsi tried to get reporters to cover a story, the newspapers would be skeptical or even angry and might pass on the news.

Similarly, if you use your brand to get access to advertising inventory, set expectations up front about the potential size and length of the relationship. If you sign a $10,000 ad buy and promise $1 million of spend in the next month if certain metrics are achieved, you should be ready to commit to the larger spend if the numbers are hit.

As an agency, we frequently get invited to requests for proposals (RFPs) as one of numerous agencies a brand asks to pitch them. There are certain well-known brands that have garnered a reputation for running unprofessional and unscrupulous RFPs. In some cases, they are indiscriminate about who they invite to the RFP, such that there may be 50 agencies competing. In others, they run RFPs that appear to be "fishing expeditions," during which they get lots of free ideas and advice from the competing agencies and then end up sticking with their current agency (and passing along a lot of great ideas to that agency). Over time, these brands become like the boy who cried wolf, and savvy agencies just ignore their RFPs. It's important to avoid this sort of reputation, as the unfair brand access advantage will quickly go away!

UNFAIR BRAND ADVANTAGE #3: DISCOUNTED MARKETING

My agency attends a lot of trade shows. Trade shows can be amazingly beneficial to our business in terms of learning and connections, or they can be a colossal waste of time. Typically speaking, the shows cost at least $2,500–$10,000 to attend, and with travel and food, the cost can easily exceed $5,000 per team member and a few days out of the office where team members can't fully focus on their work. So we reject most trade show offers simply because we don't believe we'll get ROI from our time and money. That said, if we do attend, we measure the ROI based on the number of leads garnered and sales revenue contracted.

I've noticed that trade shows generally use two methods to convince potential attendees of the value of their show.

First, they promote a list of big-name speakers that will be presenting content, and second, they emphasize the prominent brands that have sponsored the event.

Imagine you work for a digital marketing agency, and you have to choose between two conferences. Which one would you choose?

- **Conference A:** Sponsored by Google and Facebook with a keynote from the CEO of LinkedIn and the VP of marketing at Amazon.
- **Conference B:** Sponsored by Bob Smith Marketing with a keynote from the CEO of a marketing technology company you've never heard of.

Of course you'd choose Conference A. If Google and Facebook think this conference is important enough to pay to sponsor and Amazon and LinkedIn are sending senior executives to speak, this must be a big deal, right?

This brings us to a secret that a lot of people don't know. Major brands often pay a deeply discounted price—and sometimes pay nothing at all—to be sponsors of trade shows, as well as other forms of paid advertising. A good brand doesn't just benefit the company. It also benefits any company that can associate itself with that brand, as some of the prominence of the brand is transferred to the associating company.

As a result, brands can often negotiate discounts simply by allowing a partner to mention the brand in their marketing campaigns. Here are a few examples of where this can benefit the brand:

- Trade shows will routinely offer major brands discounts of 50 percent or more off their sponsorship packages, expecting that the involvement of the brand will bring in many other sponsors and attendees.
- Service providers (agencies, developers, recruiters) will charge less to established brands in exchange for permission to mention them as clients in their sales pitches.
- Publishers will offer brands discounted advertising, again as a way to boost sales to other advertisers.

CASPER: COMBINING DATA, EXPERTISE AND BRAND TO MAKE MONEY ON ADVERTISING

If you're like me, every few weeks you get a packet of coupons mailed to you. Each coupon is printed on two-sided, light paper, and the offers are almost always local service providers like painters, closet organizers, pizza joints, and driveway pavers. A direct marketing company goes out and sells space in their mailer to each of these advertisers. The advertisers benefit from sharing the cost of the mailing with dozens of other advertisers, as well as the brand of the direct mail company. Consumers recognize that the mailing will have a lot of coupons in it, and they are perhaps more inclined to open it than if they just got a letter from one paving company.

Over the last couple of years, I've started to see a different type of direct mail coupon pack arrive in my mail. Instead of a direct mail company organizing the mailer, the organizer is one of the advertisers. In particular, I noticed some mailings from Casper, the "mattress in a box" company, that included advertisers from other online retailers.

While I couldn't find any news reporting to validate my theory, I suspect that Casper has done three very smart things here. First, they created an unfair data advantage by rigorously understanding the ROI of direct mail. Second, they hired experts who had specific direct mail expertise. And last, they leveraged their brand, data, and expertise to entice other advertisers to pay them to be included in their direct mailings (or, at a minimum, Casper paid less for their share of the cost due to their prominent brand).

So now, instead of paying 75 cents to be included in a direct mailing filled with 30 other brands, Casper might actually be able to get their message delivered and make a profit on the mailing. That's a pretty amazingly unfair advantage!

UNFAIR BRAND ADVANTAGE #4: ATTRACTING TOP TALENT

While robots, algorithms, and smart machinery continue to encroach on jobs previously done exclusively by humans, we are a long way away from human-free marketing. Indeed, as technology's importance grows in marketing, the need to find humans who know how to program and run the machines is only increasing. Getting the best people to join your marketing team is crucial to your success. If you have a great brand, using that brand reputation to attract top talent is yet another unfair advantage.

I believe people choose job opportunities based on five factors, which I have created the mnemonic SCORE to represent. These are:

- **Stability:** Is the company going to be around for a long time, and can I expect the culture and the people to be relatively consistent?
- **Compensation:** How much money and stock am I being offered?
- **Opportunity:** Is there room for me to grow, learn new things, and be promoted?
- **Responsibility:** What am I going to be doing every day?
- **Environment:** Will I like the culture? Will I be excited to come to work every day?

I've generally found that employees early in their career are most concerned about stability and compensation (just getting a job that pays the rent is exciting!), whereas more senior employees focus on, to use Maslow's term, self-actualization, like opportunity, responsibility, and environment.

Established brands can use their brand value and reputation to make their job offers highly attractive to both junior and senior candidates. For junior candidates, brands can emphasize their history and reputation to assuage fears that the business might be on shaky ground or that the culture might be in flux. Candidates may also value the stock offered by the brand more than that from a startup, assuming that the chance that the stock ends up "in the money" is higher for an established brand.

For senior candidates, an established brand may be attractive in that the responsibility given to the candidate may be more helpful to their future job prospects (being VP of marketing at Ford is likely going to seem more impressive to a potential employer than being VP of marketing at a company no one has ever heard of).

For many job candidates, regardless of tenure, there's a sense of having "made it" when they get an offer at a brand they admire. We all want to make our parents proud, and what parent wouldn't want to brag about their child who is doing great things at Google, Morgan Stanley, or American Airlines?

One of the luxuries of building a great brand is that the brand doesn't have to be as innovative or risk-taking as an upstart company. This applies equally to product launches as it does to hiring. An established brand can wait until a new category is emerging before it decides to invest in (or often acquire) that category, relying on its brand reputation to help it quickly build up market share. With employees, brands can wait until a person has established their bona-fides at lesser-known companies and then only recruit the cream of the crop to join their organizations.

I'm a fan of college sports, and I see this play out all the time. A young coach gets their first head-coaching job at a small school that never competes for championships. After a few years, the team starts to make headlines, unexpect-edly defeating some heavyweights that have better recruits, higher-paid coaches, bigger stadiums, and better TV con-tracts. Suddenly, the unknown coach is a hot commodity, and one of the established brand-name programs offers them a big salary to join the big league. The rich get richer, whether we are talking about a college football team or a leading brand!

Of course, all of this assumes that the brand reputation is something that is attractive to candidates. A big brand that is constantly being outflanked by upstarts and seems to be going in the wrong direction will see their ability to recruit great talent quickly diminish. A brand that has a culture of politics, laziness, or other bad traits will suffer the same fate. Job candidates today have tools like Glassdoor and PayScale that provide them with unvarnished insider reviews of companies. In other words, the work culture cannot be fabricated by the recruiting department. If the messaging on the hiring page is effusive about collaboration and inclusiveness but the reviews on Glassdoor suggest otherwise, the company will struggle to find good candidates.

So to be clear, candidates don't just automatically default to a brand over a startup. As noted by my SCORE mnemonic, candidates look at numerous factors when choosing to work at a company. That said, **having a great brand will break a lot of ties in favor of the brand over the unknown entity. Every great candidate that you win can be the difference between good and great marketing!**

WAIT! WHAT IF I'M NOT A BIG BRAND YET?

If you run marketing at an established brand, the preceding pages may have given you some ideas to drive more growth by exploiting your brand advantage. But what if you are just starting out and don't have much (or any) brand? At this point, you may be feeling a little sick to your stomach, knowing that your brand competitors have a lot of unfair advantages in their direct response marketing. It's worth remembering at this point that every company was once a startup and didn't have a brand advantage. So these big brands found a way to grow their businesses, at least to a point, without being established brands.

Emerging brands do have a few advantages that they can use to counter the power of bigger brands.

TAKE BIGGER RISKS

The downside of a great brand is that once you've established the brand, it is hard to take risks. As Clayton Christensen pointed out in *The Innovator's Dilemma*, established companies have huge incentives to avoid risk. As a result, they often miss out on growth opportunities because they are afraid of hurting their established business. Most brands flee any risk or controversy and instead do everything they can to protect their brand.

As a startup without a brand, you can take more risks simply because you have no brand to destroy! Hiring controversial brand ambassadors, running edgy ads, advertising on controversial websites—all of these are opportunities to take risks that may pay off and that your brand competitors are unlikely to act on.

A good example of this "nothing to lose" strategy is the launch video produced by Dollar Shave Club. Dollar Shave Club is a mail-order provider of affordable razors. At launch, they were up against well-funded, large brands—in particular Gillette and Schick. So rather than a standard launch that included a press release and a professional website, the company created an edgy video. The video starts like this (warning: profanity ahead!):

> "Hi. I'm Mike—founder of dollarshave.com. What is dollarshave.com? Well, for a dollar a month, we send high-quality razors right to your door. Yeah. A dollar. Are the blades any good? No. Our blades are fucking great."[10]

At last count, this video has received more than 27 million views on YouTube. Dollar Shave's willingness to be controversial was a key factor in their massive success. In 2016, after only a few years in business, the company was sold to Unilever for $1 billion!

TURN STRENGTH INTO A WEAKNESS

A few years ago, we worked for an email service provider (ESP) startup that offered clients incredibly sophisticated email marketing solutions. The challenge for them, however, was twofold. First, they were a lot more expensive than the category leaders. Their product cost $6,000 per month, and the leading ESPs were charging $10 per month. Second, the leaders were actively promoting their $10 price point in all of their advertising as a primary brand benefit.

---

10   "Dollar Shave Club Video: The Script," Orama, last modified March 3, 2015, https://orama.tv/dollar-shave-club-script/.

We realized that we couldn't compete on price, so we decided to try to turn the competitors' brand strength into a weakness. We launched ads that read, "Serious about email marketing? You deserve better than a $10 solution!" The ads were a hit—so much so that the competition stopped mentioning price in their ads and our client grew significant market share.

An established brand is often an advantage, but a savvy startup may be able to turn *established* into *old* and *brand* into *boring* with the right strategy!

BUILD A BETTER PRODUCT

Part of being risk-averse is a fear of launching new products or services that might hurt the overall brand of a company. Large brands are often willing to cede a new category of product or service to a startup rather than risk losing profit or brand dilution to compete (this is well documented in *The Innovator's Dilemma*). PayPal disrupted checking while banks sat idly by and watched. Apple disrupted music. Uber and Lyft did the same for taxis, Amazon to shopping, eBay to auctions, etc. Brands have to spend a lot of time thinking about, well, their brand, which often results in less time on innovation!

New brands are birthed every year. Similarly, big brands that seemed like they were unbeatable suffer ignoble defeats to upstarts and fade away. Going up against an entrenched brand is almost always an uphill battle, but by maximizing all of your unfair advantages, it's a battle that you can win!

SUMMARIZING THE UNFAIR BRAND ADVANTAGE

Brands work because people like to find shortcuts in life. A brand helps you make a decision without straining your brain. Need to get a coffee in the morning? No need to think—get Starbucks. Need a safe car? Volvo is your answer—no research necessary.

A few years ago, a friend of mine wrote a book about usability (getting people to do what you want them to do on your website) with a title that encompasses the brand advantage: *Don't Make Me Think!* Good websites make it easy for customers to use them—the moment a customer gets confused is the moment they click away to another site.

As such, you can really think about the unfair brand advantage as the "Don't Make Me Think" advantage:

- Brands get higher CTR and higher conversion rates on direct response marketing—both online and offline—because customers gravitate toward brand advertisers. This means that brands pay less for advertising and get more sales out of each ad campaign. On online advertising platforms like Google and Facebook, a brand might pay pennies on the dollar for the same ad that a non-brand has to pay full price for because these platforms reward advertisers that get higher CTR.

- Brands get access to marketing opportunities that non-brands don', simply because sales representatives, journalists, and publishers are more willing to work with a brand than a non-brand. This means that it is easier for brands to do small test campaigns with publishers, get their PR included in news stories, and develop marketing partnerships.
- Brands often get offered deep discounts on sponsorships and advertising because the platform or trade show knows that the brand's participation in their program will drive non-brands to participate as well or attract buyers (either B2B or B2C) to their business. For example, brands may get free sponsorships of trade shows as a way to get non-brands to buy expensive sponsorship packages.
- Brands can attract top marketing talent to join their team because the marketers want to use the brand's reputation to further enhance their own marketing credentials.

All of these advantages are predicated on the assumption that the brand is living up to the promise behind the brand. As soon as the brand fails to deliver against the promise, the brand starts to fall apart, creating an opportunity for upstarts or alternative brands to gain market share. Neither building a brand nor maintaining a brand is easy, but for those companies that succeed, the unfair advantages are significant.

CHAPTER 5

YOUR UNFAIR MONEY ADVANTAGE

In the eighth century, a French town was besieged by an enemy army and was running out of food and water. It was only a matter of time before the town would need to open the gates and allow the enemy army to enter and ransack the town.

As legend tells it, a princess in the town—Lady Carcas—had an idea. She took what little food they had left and fed it to a pig, making the pig look as fat and healthy as possible. The town then threw it over the city wall, and it landed at the feet of the invaders. The enemy army, which had assumed (correctly) that they were just days away from victory, now came to a different conclusion: the town had so much food that they could literally taunt their besiegers with fat pigs!

Dismayed, the enemy retreated, and the town (now called Carcassonne in honor of the clever princess) was spared destruction (note for Monty Python fans: this story is parodied in *The Holy Grail* when the French throw livestock and produce over the castle walls at King Arthur and the Knights of the Roundtable!).

While Lady Carcas's gambit was a mirage, it serves as a great example of how money—or the appearance of money—can impact how others perceive and respond to you. Used wisely, money can give you a huge unfair marketing advantage that is almost unstoppable.

OBVIOUS MONEY ADVANTAGES

Almost everything discussed in the four prior chapters costs money. Want to build a great data activation machine? You'll need to buy technology and hire experts. Need a team of online marketing professionals to optimize your online ads? Those people don't come for free (though if you find some experts who will work for nothing, please send me their contact info!).

The more money you have, the more likely you are to exploit unfair advantages across data, knowledge, access, and brand. Without going into deep detail, here's how having money enables you to drive unfair advantage across these categories.

DATA

There are a lot of free tools that can give you great marketing insight. In particular, Google has done a fantastic job of offering marketers a very robust suite of analytic tools for free (Google Analytics, Google Trends, Google Search Console, TensorFlow, and Data Studio are great examples). Free tools, however, can only take you so far for two reasons. First, they often limit the amount of data they can ingest (storage and processing power are expensive). And second, any data interpretation tool is only as good as the person interpreting the data.

So you can get more and better insight by buying top-notch data technology and hiring the best data scientists you can find. Because top data scientists want to work with the best tools and the most data, creating a data tech unfair advantage by investing in the best tools enables you to hire the best data scientists, compounding your advantage.

KNOWLEDGE

If you have a bigger marketing budget, you can pay your marketing experts more money! As noted in the knowledge section, employees are never motivated entirely by money (remember the SCORE!), but money is always a factor for employees, and the greater the difference in compensation between two job offers, the greater the role that money plays in the ultimate decision.

One of the adages I've lived by as I built my marketing agency is this: it's better to hire one $120,000 person than two $60,000 people. It's always worth paying for top talent. So if you find a dream candidate and you are haggling with the candidate over a 5 percent difference between what she wants to be paid and what you want to pay, my recommendation is to pay up!

ACCESS

In 2019, companies spent $3.47 billion on lobbyists in the United States![11] What do lobbyists do? Provide unfair access advantages to the companies they represent. The ROI on lobbying can be massive. One study found that Fortune 100 companies got $200 of tax benefits for every dollar spent on lobbying.[12] Most of us would be happy with that sort of ROI on even our best marketing campaigns!

Suffice to say, after you've exhausted your "free" network of influence, if you can pay for access, this can drive a massive unfair advantage. While lobbyists focus on politicians in Washington, DC, there are plenty of ways for marketers to buy access. Examples include hosting lavish dinners,

---

11 Erin Duffin, "Total Lobbying Spending U.S. 1998–2020," Statista, last modified March 4, 2020, https://www.statista.com/statistics/257337/total-lobbying-spending-in-the-us/.

12 Adam Andrzejewski, "How The Fortune 100 Turned $2 Billion in Lobbying Spend Into $400 Billion of Taxpayer Cash," *Forbes*, last modified 14 May 2020, https://www.forbes.com/sites/adamandrzejewski/2019/05/14/how-the-fortune-100-turned-2-billion-in-lobbying-spend-into-400-billion-of-taxpayer-cash/?sh=1d11a0b354ff.

golf outings, or event retreats for thought leaders in your industry or industry executives (note: I hate golf, so that one won't work on me). You can sponsor charity events that you know will be attended by important people you want to influence, or you can hire important people as consultants or give them advisory roles in your company.

There's an entire industry online called influencer marketing where you can pay famous YouTubers or Instagram stars to promote your product to their followers. Some of these influencers demand more than $100,000 for just one mention, and even with such high fees, there's a waiting list of marketers who are dying to pay them!

BRAND

Like Lady Carcas, your brand can be greatly boosted by simply being everywhere your customers are. Is there a big trade conference coming up? With unlimited brand budget, you can buy top sponsorship, have the biggest trade show booth, and host the biggest after-party. Are there a few top keywords that every customer searches for? Make sure you show up number one, regardless of the cost and ROI, to ensure that customers perceive that you are the most prominent brand.

In general, big budgets allow brands to be front and center wherever their customers are. Big brands pay for prominent placement of their products in grocery stores, multimillion-dollar naming rights deals for stadiums and sports jerseys, and positive mentions in movies (product placement). All of these strategies increase the likelihood that a brand becomes the FUD choice. While it is possible for a brand to grow without a big budget, buying your way into brand recognition is a timeless method that has worked well for many large companies.

HIDDEN UNFAIR MONEY ADVANTAGES

All the ideas I've described are straightforward ways to use money to gain advantage. As such, your competitors are likely to figure these out pretty quickly, thereby nullifying any advantage you hope to gain. Top marketers, however, have other tricks up their sleeve that enable them to leverage money in less obvious ways. Specifically, there are three unfair money advantages that you can apply if you have more money than the competition.

HIDDEN UNFAIR MONEY ADVANTAGE #1: LOSING MONEY TO MAKE MONEY

When you are shopping for a product, especially an expensive one, you compare prices, right? If you could save $1,000 on a $10,000 purchase, you'd happily pay less and pocket the savings. Sure, in some cases, you might pay a little more to support your local merchant, or to buy from a store that has a stellar reputation for great customer service, but generally speaking, customers (both consumers and businesses) are very price sensitive.

The busiest week of shopping occurs during the week after Thanksgiving—Black Friday and Cyber Monday. During this time period, merchants offer consumers incredible deals to get them to visit their store or online site. The term "doorbuster" is often applied to these deals, and the term is often quite literal. The deals offered are so low that consumers wait in line for hours and sometimes smash windows and doors to get into a store before the doorbuster is sold out.

From a merchant perspective, the hope is that by offering a few crazy deals below cost, the bargains will drive consumers to their store, where they will also buy lots of other products that drive positive margin for the merchant.

This technique is known as a loss-leader strategy. In addition to Black Friday doorbusters, there are many other instances where merchants employ this strategy:

- **Store openings** When a new retail location opens in a town, the store may offer discounted products or services to encourage customers to try them out and hopefully become repeat customers.
- **Free trials:** Offering a free sample, deeply discounted

first order, or limited-time free subscription is a very common way to acquire customers for repeat purchase items, such as a meal kit subscriptions, mobile apps (think Headspace, for example), or streaming entertainment services (Netflix, for example).

· **Product bundling:** In exchange for a minimum purchase amount or buying a specific combination of products, the merchant might give away another product for free or way below cost.

A loss-leader strategy is very powerful—so much so that it might even be illegal to employ it. Though rare, the Federal Trade Commission (FTC) has noted that a company might be violating federal antitrust laws when "below-cost pricing allows a dominant competitor to knock its rivals out of the market and then raise prices to above-market levels for a substantial time," though the FTC is also quick to note that "although the FTC examines claims of predatory pricing carefully, courts, including the Supreme Court, have been skeptical of such claims."[13]

While I'm not a lawyer, my interpretation of this statement is that it is highly unlikely that a loss-leader strategy would be considered an antitrust violation. Note that the definition requires a *dominant* competitor with *intent to* "*knock*

---

13   "Predatory or Below-Cost Pricing," Federal Trade Commission, accessed April 7, 2021, https://
       www.ftc.gov/tips-advice/competition-guidance/guide-antitrust-laws/single-firm-conduct/
       predatory-or-below-cost.

out" its rivals who then raises *prices to above-market levels* for a *substantial time*. That is a high bar! Still, the fact that selling at a loss could potentially result in antitrust scrutiny tells you how powerful this strategy is.

Having a lot of money in the bank is important for a loss-leader strategy because you need to be able to sustain losses from your customer during the loss-leader period. If it costs you $500 to buy a TV and you are selling it to consumers for $250, you lose $250 on every TV. If you sell 100,000 TVs this way, you are now down $25 million, so you need at least that much money on hand to make this strategy work.

From a marketing perspective, having the cash to employ a loss-leader strategy gives you a substantial advantage over the competition. Imagine that you and a competitor sell the same products, and both of you are running ads on Google. Recall that the auction-based pricing on Google ranks advertisers based on two factors: CPC and CTR. You are offering customers a free blue widget on their first order, and the competition is not. The two ads look like this:

Your Ad:

Get a Free Blue Widget ($20 Value)!
Try us out for free. The first 10,000 new customers get a free blue widget!

Your Competitor's Ad:

The Best Blue Widgets
We sell the finest blue widgets, starting at
$15. Order today and save!

Because of your awesome loss-leader promotion, your CTR
is 20 percent, while your competitor is only getting a 5 percent CTR. That means to win the top result on the Google
search engine results page (SERP), you only need to pay
25 percent as much per click as the competition (and the
competition has to pay four times your bid).

Moreover, the conversion rate on your offer is 20 percent,
and the competitor only gets a 4 percent conversion rate.
So after someone clicks through, you are five times more
effective at signing them up as a new customer. Combine
your four-times CPC advantage with your five-times conversion rate advantage, and your customer acquisition cost
(CAC) is 20 times better than the competition!

To be clear, you still need to make money for your business. For the loss-leader model to work, you have to convert
many of these free trials into paying customers. Assuming
you offer customers good prices, quality products, and great
customer service, getting that new customer to choose you
over the competition may be the start of a long and profitable relationship for your business. Remember, you were

only able to execute this strategy because you had more money in the bank than your competitor!

There's also a potential PR and branding benefit to a loss-leader strategy. When companies offer below-cost or free deals, these promotions often get picked up by the news media or by websites focused on bargains. Starbucks, for example, offers free coffee on National Coffee Day and gets significant media coverage of the offering. Burger King gives away a free Whopper on Valentine's Day (who needs roses?), and the press eats it up (perhaps literally).

When TOMS shoes launched, they promised consumers that for every purchase, they'd donate one pair of shoes to a person in need. To date, they've donated more than 100 million pairs. No doubt this was done in large part because the founders truly wanted to help needy people, but the PR from this has been enormous. I'll note that this is not a loss-leader per se because TOMS is making enough money on the pair of shoes the consumer buys to cover the cost of the free pair, but it is still an example of losing some profit to drive a marketing advantage.

HIDDEN UNFAIR MONEY ADVANTAGE #2: PLAYING THE LONG GAME

From 1996 (when Amazon went public) to 2003, Amazon didn't have a single year where the company made a profit.

From 2004 to 2015, the best year of profit for the company was 2010, when it made $1.1 billion of profit on revenue of $34 billion. Then in 2016, profits started to grow massively, from $2.3 billion in 2016 to $11.6 billion in 2019 (on revenue of $280.5 billion).[14]

This long road to profitability was no accident. Amazon could have built a very nice (and profitable) business selling books, CDs, and electronics. But instead of making a profit every year, Amazon aggressively reinvested in their business, adding more product categories and their own line of electronics (like the Kindle or Fire), building out cloud hosting, creating robotic warehouses and a delivery service, producing movies, offering free shipping, and so on.

All of these offerings were designed to increase Amazon's LTV among consumers and businesses. Great companies understand that repeat customers spend more, require less customer service, are more profitable, and are more likely to refer others.

From a marketing perspective, optimizing for LTV gives companies like Amazon an unfair advantage similar to what we saw with a loss-leader strategy. In Amazon's case, a study from 2013 suggested that the average Amazon Prime

---

14   "Amazon Net Income by Year: FY 1996 to 2020," Dazeinfo, last modified February 3, 2021, https://dazeinfo.com/2019/11/06/amazon-net-income-by-year-graphfarm/.

customer spent $1,340 a year with Amazon.[15] I'm going to assume that this number significantly underestimates the true LTV of an Amazon customer because Amazon sells a lot more stuff today than it did in 2013, and the average Amazon customer probably shops with Amazon for five years or more.

So for the sake of argument, let's assume that the average customer now spends $2,000 a year and sticks around for just three years. That's a total value to Amazon of $6,000. Assuming that Amazon makes 5 percent profit from this customer, the company will make $300 of profit per customer.

Now imagine that you are running marketing at Amazon, and it is "back to school" season. One of the products you sell is a set of a dozen pencils, with a total cost to the consumer of $3. If you were optimizing your advertising to be profitable on the sale of this one pencil set, you could pay no more than 15 cents for this purchase (5 percent). If, however, your data told you that 10 percent of new customers who bought this pencil set would end up signing up for Amazon Prime, you could pay $15 and still make $15 of profit on this customer (one in ten customers would end up becoming an Amazon Prime customer with $300 of net profit).

15 Brendan Mathews, "What's a Prime Member Worth to Amazon.com?" *The Motley Fool*, last modified February 20, 2018, https://www.fool.com/investing/general/2014/04/21/whats-a-prime-member-worth-to-amazoncom.aspx.

In this scenario, even if a competitor wanted to spend 100 percent of the cost of the pencil set to get a $3 sale, Amazon could still pay five times as much and be profitable. Thus, **companies that can accurately calculate their LTV and then have the financial means to acquire customers based on the anticipated LTV can make marketing investments that their competitors could never make.**

Every day on my way to work, I walk past two stores. One is Starbucks. Though it's a mega-chain, when you go inside, you somehow feel that this is *your local* Starbucks. There's a big sign that says "Your Barista is..." There are comfy chairs, soft music, and very friendly staff.

Directly across the street from this Starbucks is an art gallery. The gallery appears to sell cheap mass-produced sculptures, starving-artist paintings, and knock-off art prints. I've been walking past this store for years now, and they've had the exact same banner out front. It reads, "ART GALLERY CLOSING. 50%–80% OFF."

I should point out that both of these stores are located in a touristy section of San Francisco, and both are within 100 yards of one of San Francisco's famous cable car lines.

Of course, while tourists might frequent both an art gallery and Starbucks, locals like myself would never dream of strolling into a tourist trap and coming home with a $2,500 bronze sculpture of a unicorn.

More to the point of this story is that any local like me would especially avoid this art gallery simply because we know that it is a scam operation. Obviously, the "50–80 percent off" sale is a con designed to make one-time visitors (e.g., tourists) think that they have discovered an incredible deal. Locals who see the sign for months know better.

The Starbucks-art gallery dichotomy reminded me that not all internet businesses care about LTV simply because some online businesses can't really expect more than a one-time interaction with the customer, not unlike an art gallery in a tourist area.

Consider, for example, an online lead generator. Let's say you are marketing mortgages. Each time you get someone to fill out your lead form, a mortgage company pays you $20 for the right to call that potential client. You create a website called Get-A-Great-Mortgage.com, and you advertise it on Google Ads, banner ads, etc.

As soon as someone comes to your website, you have one objective: get them to fill out a form so that you get your $20. You could care less whether the experience after they hit "submit" is good or bad; after all, they can only fill out the offer once (or, more specifically, you can only get paid once), and what are the odds that anyone would refer their friends to a mortgage form?

In such an example, the online lead generator is no different than the art gallery. You only need to satisfy the customer for a very short period of time. Once you make your one-time fee, whether the customer experience falls apart later on doesn't matter to you.

On the flip side, businesses like etailers are like Starbucks. Imagine what would happen if you bought a book on Amazon and it arrived at your house two weeks later than promised and was damaged, and then Amazon refused to exchange it? You'd tell five friends how horrible your experience was. You might post some bad reviews online, and you certainly would never shop at Amazon again.

Few retail businesses could survive long term without repeat customers and positive word of mouth simply because retailers with better LTV will eventually be able to spend more to acquire new customers than retailers with bad LTV. Over time, the high-LTV retailer will maintain its existing base and grow its new customers, while the bad-LTV retailer will die a slow death.

Judging from the fact that my local art gallery's "going out of business" sale has now lasted at least one year, I'm confident that you can, in fact, create a decent business—offline or online—through one-time sales. But the art gallery is a solitary store, whereas Starbucks has tens of thousands of locations.

Translation: running a business without LTV can be profitable, but it can't be scalable. Lead generators can only grow by moving into new verticals. Growing new businesses is costly, time-consuming, and labor-intensive. An etailer like Amazon grows simply by adding to its existing business (new products) and through loyal repeat business. This is less costly and more profitable than the "new business of the week" model.

Ultimately, the barriers to entry for a multi-purchase, large LTV business are much greater than a business that only gets one purchase from a customer. I know I would get crushed if I tried to open up a coffee shop across from Starbucks, but I'd have greater confidence going head to head with Cheap Sculptures R Us. Similarly, setting up a lead generation business is reasonably easy (which explains why there are tens of thousands of affiliates doing just that), but growing a successful etailer is much more challenging.

HIDDEN UNFAIR MONEY ADVANTAGE #3: LOW PRICING

Whatever product or service you sell, there are likely three types of competitors in your industry: established brands, low-price leaders, and everyone else. I refer to companies in the "everyone else" category as "the muddy middle." Lacking a strong brand, these companies can't win on FUD or brand reputation, and lacking low prices, they can't win on economics.

Many years ago, the general manager of the Orlando Magic basketball team (whose team at that time was a perennial loser) quipped, "We can't win at home. We can't win on the road. As general manager, I just can't figure out where else to play." This is how it must feel for companies in the muddy middle.

As a marketer, you often don't have control over product sourcing or pricing. Hopefully, however, you can exert some influence over these decisions and explain to the rest of your company why it is important to either win on price or win on brand.

The first thing to explain to your company is that pricing is relative and fluid. A $500 TV is only a bargain if every other TV costs at least $750. Of course, if a competitor suddenly cuts the price of their TV to $400, your $500 TV is no longer a bargain.

More and more, customers have complete access to pricing when they shop. This is evident when you walk into a supermarket, where the pricing signs not only mention the item price but the unit price (e.g., 2.8 cents per sheet of toilet paper); on Amazon, where you can quickly sort by price; or on Google ads, where a shopper can review four or more ads at once for the same product search. In the old days (the 1990s?), a consumer could walk onto a car dealership lot, the salesperson could claim the lowest price available, and the consumer would have limited resources to fact-check this claim. Today, consumers show the dealer the price they've discovered online and ask the dealer to beat it. This is known as showrooming or webrooming.[16]

I recently received a catalog from Hammacher Schlemmer in the mail and noticed an amazing change in the way the company sold products. Most of the products listed did not include the brand or model name of the product. Instead, they simply described the product itself, like "The Live Fitness Class Rower."[17] Instantly, I realized why the catalog was doing this: to prevent shoppers from entering the brand and model name into Google to search for a lower price!

This strategy, by the way, while clever, ultimately leaves Hammacher Schlemmer in the muddy middle (if you browse their catalog, you'll see that there are plenty of ways to figure out the brand and model name and do a Google or Amazon search!).

16 Humayun Khan, "Consumers Are Showrooming and Webrooming Your Business, Here's What Tat Means and What You Can Do About It," *Shopify*, last modified June 7, 2018, https://www.shopify.com/retail/119920451-consumers-are-showrooming-and-webrooming-your-business-heres-what-that-means-and-what-you-can-do-about-it.

17 "Hammacher Schlemmer - Select Gifts 2020 - Page 10-11," Hammacher Schlemmer, accessed April 7, 2021, https://view.publitas.com/hammacher-schlemmer/select-gifts-2020/page/10-11.

Rather than attempting to deter customers from price shopping, a better approach is to simply do everything you can to be price competitive. There are a few ways to achieve this goal. First, you can offer a price-match guarantee. If a customer finds a lower price (usually within a certain amount of time), you refund them the difference. This reduces price shopping, and many customers won't go through the work of doing the price check anyway!

A second idea is to constantly monitor competitor pricing and react quickly to any price reductions by lowering your prices further. This is such a common practice in some industries that software has been built to do this automatically for retailers.

Indeed, a few years ago, two booksellers were both using such software on Amazon to reduce their price by one cent every time a competitor lowered their prices. In this instance, however, both booksellers mistakenly set their programs to *increase* price by one cent every time a rival increased price. This created an infinite feedback loop and ended up with one seller offering a biology book about flies for $23,698,655.93![18] Don't do that. But do consider carefully watching for price changes.

The last technique is to find efficiency in your business that

---

18   Olivia Solon, "How a Book about Flies Came to be Priced $24 Million on Amazon," *Wired*, last modified April 27, 2011, https://www.wired.com/2011/04/amazon-flies-24-million/.

enables you to offer better prices. Wish is a mobile app that offers consumers bargain prices on thousands of products. They are able to do so because they source their products directly from manufacturers, largely in China. As of 2019, they were valued by investors at over $11 billion and had more than 70 million active shoppers.[19] This is a great example of a company that scaled simply because they found a way to sell stuff for less than competitors.

Efficiency that reduces prices, by the way, is not limited to B2C companies. B2B businesses can find ways to cut costs and pass the savings on to customers. Examples include outsourcing or rural sourcing, offering different solutions and service levels that enable lower cost offerings, and offering discounts in exchange for longer-term commitments.

To be clear, just because you could lower your prices doesn't mean you should. There are instances where customers associate low prices with low quality and specifically choose a more expensive solution. Also, unless you are executing a loss-leader or LTV strategy, you shouldn't lower prices to the point that you are losing money on orders. If you have established a brand in your category, you may not need to cut prices to win business.

---

19   Connie Loizos, "What Will a Wish IPO Look Like? We May Know Soon," *TechCrunch*, last modified September 1, 2020, https://techcrunch.com/2020/09/01/what-will-a-wish-ipo-look-like-seems-well-find-out-sooner-than-later/.

That said, if you can become the low-cost leader and still make a profit, you need to exploit this advantage in every aspect of your marketing. Put your price front and center in all of your ad copy (higher CTR and lower CPC in the case of a bidding system like Google Ads), create PR campaigns that explain to journalists how you are able to sell for so much less than the competition (especially if there's an interesting story behind it), and prominently display the price on the product packaging if you are selling in retail locations. You may even consider incorporating your low-cost leader status into your branding. Payless, a discount shoe retailer, used the brand slogan, "You could pay more, but why?" to make the argument to consumers that their shoes were just as good as the designer brands but cost way less.

What If I'm in the Muddy Middle?

Sometimes, no matter how hard you try, you end up in the muddy middle. Maybe this is because you are a new company and haven't had time to build a brand or you don't have enough funding to create economies of scale to lower your prices. Or maybe your business just isn't structured in a way to ever be a big brand or a low-cost leader. If this describes your business, the last few pages probably didn't sit well with you.

The good news is that there are ways to grow your business

even if it appears you are in the muddy middle. There are three techniques that I'd recommend: reposition your brand, reposition your market, and reposition your marketing.

The first technique is to reposition your brand. Specifically, to follow this rule, if you can't be number one in a category, create a category you can be number one in.[20] When GoPro launched their video camera in 2004, there were dozens of large, well-funded competitors like Sony and Panasonic that dominated the video camera market.

So rather than describing their product as a video camera, the company invented the concept of an "action camera"—a camera specifically designed for action sports like surfing and skiing. By creating this new category, the company could rely on their brand leadership to grow revenue instead of deeply discounting their cameras in an attempt to be the low-cost leader.

The second approach is to reposition your solution to target a niche audience. There are hundreds of CRM companies trying to compete with Salesforce (and mostly losing market share), but there are only a few companies like Fishbowl that have built a CRM solution specifically for restaurants or WiseAgent's CRM for real estate brokers. While every company wants to acquire as many customers as possible,

---

20   Al Ries and Laura Ries,.*The 22 Immutable Laws of Branding: How to Build a Product Or Service Into a World-Class Brand* (New York: HarperCollins, 2002).

competing against an entrenched, deeply funded giant is often a losing battle, especially if you don't have financial resources to go on the offensive against the incumbent.

For this reason, many savvy companies realize that it's better to be a big fish in a small pond than a small fish in a big pond and thus change their solution and focus to be narrowly tailored to a specific set of potential customers. In *The Innovator's Dilemma*, Clayton Christensen details how Toyota launched in the US market by offering a subcompact car. The big American motor companies saw this car as a low-margin, niche product and were happy to cede this category to Toyota and instead focus on high-margin categories like full-size cars and trucks. Over time, however, Toyota used their success in subcompacts to enter into more and more categories and eventually became one of the top car companies in the US.

The last strategy is to reposition your marketing. As noted, there are certain marketing channels that are only effective if you are a leading brand and don't need to compete on price or if you are a low-cost leader. Examples include advertising on Google and Amazon and in-store placements (like supermarkets or electronics stores). In these environments, the customer has instant access to comparative pricing data, so it is very hard to get sales if you are in the muddy middle.

Instead of waging a losing war on these channels, take the

fight to channels where you have a better chance of success (e.g., channels that don't provide comparative pricing information). This could include trade show sponsorships, billboards, direct mail, SEO, TV, radio, or PR. If you can convince a customer to go directly to your store or website without even researching the competition, you may be able to build a successful business while stuck in the muddy middle!

SUMMARIZING THE MONEY ADVANTAGE

Money is not a cure-all. In 2019, a content company called Quibi raised more than $1.75 billion to create a streaming media platform designed for mobile phones. When the service launched, the shows it offered consumers received terrible reviews. Very few consumers signed up for the service, and the company closed less than a year after launch. Quibi is not an anomaly—business history is filled with case studies of companies spending massive sums of capital only to see customers shun and even mock their products or services.

That said, given the choice between having too much money and not enough, I'll take the money! Money enables companies to sell products for less, take a long view on profitability, and create attractive incentives to get customers to switch to their offering. Money can mean bigger marketing budgets, better data analysis, and better marketing experts.

Companies that have more money than the competition should leverage this advantage at every opportunity. Their competitors, meanwhile, must come up with creative solutions to combat this advantage, often by rethinking the company brand, product, or marketing to avoid direct conflict with their better-funded competitors.

FINAL THOUGHTS

ET TU, BRUTUS?

My high school's newspaper—*The West Side Story*—prints an inspirational quote from each graduating senior in their last edition of the year. Having just completed Shakespeare's *Julius Caesar* in 12th grade English, when I graduated, I chose this quote: "The fault, dear Brutus, is not in our stars, but in ourselves."

On one level, this quote is about blaming others (or bad luck or the universe) for your problems. On another, it's about owning your own destiny. Indeed, the line right before this famous quote is this: "Men at some times are masters of their fates."

Imagine Brutus as a modern marketer. Faced with a competitor with a bigger marketing budget, a more prominent brand, and influential connections, he would have given up. "The stars are aligned against me! Why bother trying to fight against inevitable defeat?"

Poor Brutus! If only he had discovered his company's unfair marketing advantages instead of wallowing in defeat. He may have countered that large marketing budget with a smarter budget, relying on better data analysis and proprietary ad buys to achieve better impact for less money. He may have used his own network to find brand advocates and influencers to put his brand on the same level as his foe. Or perhaps he would have relied on his team's specific marketing experience and knowledge to build out marketing strategies that dramatically took market share away from the incumbent.

Whether you are the biggest player in your industry or the youngest and smallest startup, you will maximize the impact of your marketing by seeking out and exploiting your unfair advantages. To not do so is lazy at best and could be fatal to your future business prospects.

You will share with your competitors all the standard techniques that marketers learn in college or through an "introduction to marketing" guide. These techniques work well enough, but they won't get you breakthrough results. Everyone already knows about "the four P's," that you should probably be advertising on Google and Facebook, and that you need clear calls to actions and benefit statements to describe your product or service. Again, this is stuff that you should definitely do, but it doesn't give you an advantage over the competition.

Unfair marketing, by contrast, means discovering data, knowledge, access, brand, and money advantages that aren't easily replicable (or known) by other companies. Perfect these techniques, and your rivals will be powerless to respond directly (though, if they are reading this too, they'll have their own schemes that you will not be able to copy either). Good marketers study all the marketing 101 basics and follow marketing best practices to execute their marketing campaigns. Great marketers see the standard best practices as a launching point to go forth and discover unique and proprietary strategies that result in world domination!

Life is unfair. You can take this statement as a negative, as in "I had to share my cupcakes with that kid even though he didn't share his cupcakes yesterday," or you can see this as an amazing opportunity to identify the unfair advantages that you have that others don't and exploit them. I believe you'll have a lot more fun—and success—if you choose the latter!

GLOSSARY

- **AI:** Artificial Intelligence (AI) is intelligence demonstrated by machines, unlike the natural intelligence displayed by humans and animals.
- **Algorithm:** A step-by-step procedure to solve logical and mathematical problems.
- **Alpha-beta account structure:** The alpha-beta structure breaks keywords into two different campaigns—alpha and beta. Alpha campaigns contain exact-match keywords that are strong-performing search queries. Beta campaigns contain broad-match modifier (BMM) keywords. These give advertisers more control than broad-match keywords and are more inclusive than phrase-match keywords.
- **Alphas:** Software testing used to identify bugs before releasing the product to the public.
- **API:** An application programming interface (API) is a

computing interface that defines interactions between multiple software intermediaries. It defines the kinds of calls or requests that can be made, how to make them, the data formats that should be used, the conventions to follow, etc. It can also provide extension mechanisms so that users can extend existing functionality in various ways and to varying degrees.[21]

- **Attribution:** The identification of a set of user actions (events or touchpoints) that contribute in some manner to a desired outcome and the assignment of a value to each of these events.[22]
- **Awareness:** The ability to directly know and perceive, feel, or be cognizant of events.
- **Betas:** Software testing performed by a select number of real users outside the company.
- **BI: Business Intelligence** (BI) comprises the strategies and technologies used by enterprises for the data analysis of business information. BI technologies provide historical, current, and predictive views of business operations. Common functions of BI technologies include reporting, online analytical processing, analytics, dashboard development, data mining, process mining, complex event processing, business perfor-

---

21   "API," Wikipedia, last modified March 27, 2021, https://en.wikipedia.org/wiki/Applications_Programming_Interface.

22   Lisa Levine and Tiffany Kelly, "A-Z Glossary of Digital Advertising Terms," Lineup Systems, accessed April 7, 2021, https://www.lineup.com/hubfs/A-Z%20Glossary%20of%20Digital%20Advertising%20Terms.pdf?hsLang=en.

mance management, benchmarking, text mining, predictive analytics, and prescriptive analytics.[23]

- **Call tracking:** A technology that can enable the pay-per-call, pay-per-minute or pay-per-lead business model, allowing the tracking of phone calls to be associated with performance-based advertising such as Google Ads, SEO services, display and electronic direct marketing, and supplying additional analytic information about the phone calls themselves.[24]

- **CCPA:** The California Consumer Privacy Act (CCPA) is a state statute intended to enhance privacy rights and consumer protection for residents of California in the United States.

- **CDP:** A customer data platform (CDP) is a type of packaged software that creates a persistent, unified customer database that is accessible to other systems. Data is pulled from multiple sources, cleaned, and combined to create a single customer profile. This structured data is then made available to other marketing systems.[25]

- **Cookie:** A small piece of data stored on the user's computer by the web browser while browsing a website. Cookies were designed to be a reliable mechanism for websites to remember stateful information (such as

23   "Business Intelligence," Wikipedia, last modified April 3, 2021, https://en.wikipedia.org/wiki/Business_intelligence.

24   "Call-Tracking Software," Wikipedia, last modified January 8, 2021, https://en.wikipedia.org/wiki/Call-tracking_software.

25   "What Is a CDP?" Teradata, accessed April 7, 2021, https://www.teradata.com/Glossary/What-is-a-CDP.

items added in the shopping cart in an online store) or to record the user's browsing activity (including clicking particular buttons, logging in, or recording which pages were visited in the past).[26]

- **CPA:** Cost per action (CPA), sometimes also misconstrued in marketing environments as cost per acquisition, is an online advertising measurement and pricing model referring to a specified action—for example a sale, click, or form submitted (e.g., contact request, newsletter sign-up, registration, etc.)

- **CPC:** Cost per click (CPC) is calculated by dividing the advertising cost by the number of clicks generated by an advertisement. The basic formula is cost per click ($) = advertising cost ($)/ads clicked (#).

- **CPI:** Cost per install (CPI) is calculated by dividing the advertising cost by the number of installs of an app. The basic formula is cost per install ($) = advertising cost ($)/app installs (#).

- **CPM:** Cost per thousand impressions (CPM) is a term used in traditional advertising media selection, as well as online advertising and marketing related to web traffic. It refers to the cost of traditional advertising, internet marketing, or email advertising campaigns, where advertisers pay each time an ad is displayed.[27]

---

26   "HTTP Cookie," Wikipedia, last modified April 6, 2021, https://en.wikipedia.org/wiki/HTTP_cookie.

27   "Pay-Per-Impression (PPI) Advertising Agreement," Gabor Melli's Research Knowledge Base, last modified March 13, 2021, http://www.gabormelli.com/RKB/Pay-per-Impression_Advertising_Agreement.

- **CRM:** Customer relationship management (CRM) is one of many different approaches that allows a company to manage and analyze their own interactions with their past, current, and potential customers.
- **CTR:** Click-through rate (CTR) is the ratio of users who click on a specific link to the number of total users who view a page, email, or advertisement. It is commonly used to measure the success of an online advertising campaign for a particular website as well as the effectiveness of email campaigns.[28]
- **DMP:** A data management platform (DMP) is a software platform used for collecting and managing data. It allows businesses to identify audience segments, which can be used to target specific users and contexts in online advertising campaigns.
- **ERP:** Enterprise resource planning (ERP) is the integrated management of main business processes, often in real time and mediated by software and technology.
- **First-party data:** Data collected and owned by the company itself.
- **First-touch attribution:** The first-touch model gives 100 percent of the credit to the marketing effort that drove a visitor to your website for the first time. Because it gives all the credit on the basis of a single touchpoint,

---

28 "Click Through Rate Calculator," V2 Main, accessed April 7, 2021, https://akash191095.github.io/ctr/.

it will naturally overemphasize a single part of the funnel.[29]

- **FUD:** Fear, uncertainty, and doubt (often shortened to FUD) is a disinformation strategy used in sales, marketing, PR, politics, polling, cults, and propaganda.
- **GDPR:** The General Data Protection Regulation (GDPR) is a regulation on data protection and privacy in the European Union (EU) and the European Economic Area (EEA). It also addresses the transfer of personal data outside the EU and EEA areas.[30]
- **HIPPO:** An acronym for the highest paid person's opinion or the highest paid person in the office. The acronym is used to describe the tendency for employees to defer to higher-paid employees when a decision has to be made.[31]
- **KPIs:** A performance indicator or key performance indicator (KPI) is a type of performance measurement. KPIs evaluate the success of an organization or of a particular activity (such as projects, programs, products, and other initiatives) in which it engages.[32]

---

29   "Bizible," Marketo Engage, accessed April 7, 2021, https://www.bizible.com/blog/marketing-attribution-models-complete-list.

30   "General Data Protection Regulation," Wikipedia, last modified April 7, 2021, https://en.wikipedia.org/wiki/General_Data_Protection_Regulation.

31   Ed Burns, "HiPPO (Highest Paid Person's Opinion, Highest Paid Person's Office)," WhatIs.com, last modified December 2013, https://whatis.techtarget.com/definition/HiPPOs-highest-paid-persons-opinions.

32   Devin, "Key Performance Indicators (KPIs) and Critical Success Factors (CSFs)," I Power Ideas, accessed April 7, 2021, https://www.ipowerideas.com/2019/06/03/key-performance-indicators-kpis-and-critical-success-factors-csfs/.

- **Last-touch attribution:** A model that gives the conversion credit entirely to the final touchpoint where a lead has converted from (i.e., made a purchase).
- **Lift:** In marketing, lift represents an increase in sales in response to some form of advertising or promotion. Monitoring, measuring, and optimizing lift may help a business grow more quickly.
- **Look-alikes:** A process that identifies people who look and act just like your target audience. Look-alike modeling uses machine learning to find more users who will take that action. This means your campaigns can scale to reach more people with a higher engagement rate.[33]
- **Loss-leader:** A pricing strategy where a product is sold at a loss in order to encourage customers to buy more expensive products or become long-time customers of a business.
- **LTV:** In marketing, lifetime value (LTV) is a prediction of the net profit attributed to the entire future relationship with a customer.
- **Marketing automation:** A software tool used to collect and manage marketing data about your potential customers and then automate the ongoing marketing to these prospects.
- **ML:** Machine learning is the study of computer algorithms that improve automatically through experience. Machine learning algorithms build a model based on

---

33   "Back to Basics: What is Look-Alike Modeling?" Lotame, last modified May 6, 2018, https://www.lotame.com/back-basics-look-alike-modeling/.

sample data, known as training data, in order to make predictions or decisions without being explicitly programmed to do so.[34]

- **MQL:** A marketing qualified lead (MQL) is a lead who has indicated interest in what a brand has to offer based on marketing efforts or is otherwise more likely to become a customer than other leads.[35]
- **Multi-touch attribution:** Multi-touch attribution is the identification of and assignment of value to a set of user actions that contribute in some manner to a desired outcome.
- **Normalization:** The process of creating relativity and context within your marketing database by grouping similar values into one common value. Any data field can be standardized. General examples include job title, job function, company name, industry, state, country, etc.
- **PII:** Personally identifiable information (PII) is data that can be used to identify someone. It is typically actively collected, meaning the information is provided directly by the individual.
- **POS:** While POS often refers to a point-of-sale system, it also refers to the customer-product interactions that occur close to where the actual sale of the product hap-

34 Bharath K., "12 Steps for Beginner to Pro in Data Science in 12 Months!" *Towards Data Science*, last modified December 25, 2020, https://towardsdatascience.com/12-steps-for-beginner-to-pro-in-data-science-in-12-months-c6f6ba01f96e.

35 "The Definition of a Marketing Qualified Lead (and What It's Not)," Tableau, accessed April 7, 2021, https://www.tableau.com/learn/articles/marketing-qualified-lead.

pens. The goal is to draw the customer's attention to your products and market to shoppers who are already in the store and ready to make a purchase.[36]

- **PR:** Public relations is a marketing practice that seeks to drive awareness of a business or product through news mentions.

- **Preference:** A branding strategy that seeks to convince consumers to prefer one brand over others.

- **Psychographics:** The qualitative methodology of studying consumers based on psychological characteristics and traits, such as values, desires, goals, interests, and lifestyle choices. Psychographics in marketing focuses on understanding the consumer's emotions and values so you can market more accurately.

- **Python:** A programming language that can drive automation across all of your marketing activities. It can be used to create valuable and professional-looking visualizations that enhance your marketing analysis. Python can be used to streamline data collection processes from multiple channels.[37]

- **R:** A programming language used for statistical analysis.

- **Remnant inventory:** The space that a media company has been unable to sell. For example, the leftover space

---

36   Francesca Nicasio, "Point of Sale Marketing: How to Optimize Your POS Area for Increased Sales," *Vend*, last modified April 14, 2019, https://www.vendhq.com/blog/point-of-sale-marketing/.

37   Kateryna Koidan, "Why Use Python in Marketing?" *LearnPython*, last modified May 14, 2019, https://learnpython.com/blog/why-use-python-in-marketing/.

in a newspaper or magazine that is still available close to the publishing date.[38]

- **RFP:** A request for proposal (RFP) is a document that solicits a proposal, often made through a bidding process by an agency or company interested in procurement of a commodity, service, or valuable asset, to potential suppliers to submit business proposals.[39]

- **ROI:** Return on investment (ROI) is a ratio between net profit (over a period) and cost of investment (resulting from an investment of some resources at a point in time).[40]

- **RPM:** Revenue per mille (RPM) is the estimated earnings that accrue for every 1,000 impressions received (in Latin, mille means thousand), a commonly used measurement in radio, television, newspaper, magazine, out-of-home, and online advertising.

- **SaaS:** Software as a service (SaaS) that is also known as subscribeware or rentware. It's a software licensing and delivery model in which software is licensed on a subscription basis and is centrally hosted.

- **Second-party data:** This is essentially someone else's

38 David Klein, "Difference between Premium vs. Remnant Inventory," *MacroMark*, last modified January 22, 2019, https://macromark.com/blog/difference-between-premium-vs-remnant-inventory.

39 "Request for Proposal," Wikipedia, last modified March 23, 2021, https://en.wikipedia.org/wiki/RFP.

40 Ahmed Ismail, "What is Return on Investment (ROI)? ROI Definition and Usage," *Post Journal*, last modified September 30, 2019, https://www.ipostjournal.com/what-is-return-on-investment-roi-definition-and-usage/.

first-party data. The seller collects data straight from their audience, and it all comes from one source.

- **SEM:** Search engine marketing (SEM) is a form of internet marketing that involves the promotion of websites by increasing their visibility in search engine result pages (SERPs) primarily through paid advertising.[41]
- **SEO:** Search engine optimization (SEO) is the process of improving the quality and quantity of website traffic to a website or a web page from search engines. SEO targets unpaid traffic (known as natural or organic results) rather than direct traffic or paid traffic.[42]
- **SERPs:** Search Engine Results Pages (SERPs) are the result of a user's search query and may contain URLs to relevant webpages, paid advertisements, .and multimedia objects related to the search term.
- **SMART:** An acronym that stands for specific, measurable, achievable, realistic, and timely. A SMART goal incorporates all of these criteria to help focus your efforts and increase the chances of achieving your goal.[43]
- **SMB:** Small and medium-sized business.
- **SQL:** Structured Query Language is a domain-specific language used in programming and designed for man-

41   "Search Engine Marketing," Wikipedia, last modified February 26, 2021, https://en.wikipedia.org/wiki/Search_engine_marketing.

42   "Search Engine Optimization," Wikipedia, last modified March 25, 2021, https://en.wikipedia.org/wiki/Search_engine_optimization.

43   "What is a SMART Goal?" Corporate Finance Institute, accessed April 7, 2021, https://corporatefinanceinstitute.com/resources/knowledge/other/smart-goal/.

aging data held in a relational database management system (RDBMS) or for stream processing in a relational data stream management system (RDSMS). It is particularly useful in handling structured data (i.e., data incorporating relations among entities and variables).[44]

- **Third-party data:** A data supplier (or service provider) that is not directly controlled by either the seller (first party) or the customer/buyer (second party) in a business transaction.

- **TLA:** The abbreviation TLA means three-letter abbreviation or three-letter acronym" and refers to a phrase or term represented by three letters. TLAs are widely used for speed in speech and in writing.

- **Tracking URL:** The act of archiving existing websites and tracking changes to the website over time. Many applications exist for website tracking that can be applied to many different purposes.

- **Web analytics:** The measurement, collection, analysis, and reporting of web data for purposes of understanding and optimizing web usage.

44 Lianne and Justin, "How to Download and Install SQL Server and Sample Database: Step-by-Step," *Just into Data*, last modified April 29, 2020, https://www.justintodata.com/download-install-sql-server-sample-database/.

ACKNOWLEDGMENTS

I am fortunate to be surrounded by a large community of family, friends, colleagues, and mentors who have given me so much love, wisdom, and joy. And sure, they helped me complete this book, but more importantly, they are all people who just make life more wonderful.

First, a thank you to my family: my wife, Rebecca; two boys, Zev and Sammy; parents, Bob and Donna; in-laws, Paul and Ellen; and siblings, Adam and Laura. Being related to an entrepreneur can be a tiring and trying experience, and your love, humor, and patience have enabled me to chart my own path and still have fun along the way.

To all the people at 3Q Digital in the "adolescent years" who helped me build a little consulting business into a legitimate company: Maury Domengeaux, Ron Fusco, Brian

Grabowski, Frank Lee, Will Lin, Sean Marshall, Scott Rayden, Hillary Read, Diego Rovira, Stacy Stern, and Dave Yoo.

To the next generation of 3Q who are turning performance into growth: Aaron Bart, Peter Berghoff, Ellen Corrigan, Jerry Graunke, Terry Graunke, Tari Haro, Sam Huston, Shane Kern, Victoria Ketchum, Jim Kingsbury, Stephanie Mace, Feliks Malts, Rob Murray, Troy Noard, Penny Pritzker, Laura Rodnitzky (again!), Maggie Shepherd, Linda Warnock, Tony Wiesman, and the more than 500 other 3Qers I can't fit on the page. I have always tried to work with people smarter than me. Thank you for letting me harness some of your EQ, IQ, and XQ to grow 3Q!

Thanks to all my colleagues in Silicon Valley and beyond who partnered with me, counseled me, or just gave me regular company at lunch (back when we could do such a thing): Tim Ash, David Baga, Gary Bauer, Ty Bennett, Brett Berson, Mark Berwick, Tami Bhaumik, Aron Bohlig, Gleb Budman, Pete Castaldi, Gallant Chen, Meagen Eisenberg, Adam Foroughi, Brady Fox, Bob Guccione Jr., Saar Gur, Justin Hersch, Tina Hoang-To, Loretta Jones, Noam Kedem, Pete Kim, Ani Kortikar, Andy Kurtzig, Yidienne Lai, Aileen Lee, Jason Lemkin, Eric Liaw, Alon Matas, Kunal Mehta, Rick Natsch, Ha Ngyuen, Tony Phillips, Keith Posehn, George Rosenberg, Ron Scheinderman, Christian Selchau-Hansen, Jonathan Sills, Tim Stanley, Seth Streeter, Doug Tarr, Neal

Tolaney, Lance Trebesch, Mitchell Weisman, Kevin Wilk, Michael Wolraich, Dave Yuan, and Craig Zelden.

Thank you to my friends and competitors in the digital marketing space! What a great industry I picked—so many good people ready to share knowledge, lend a hand, and play the game hard but fair. Thank you to Tom Bedecarre, David Canington, Sanjay Chadda, David Clark, Dhiren D'Souza, Eric Facas, Ryan Gibson, Bob Glazer, Larry Kim, Ben Kirschner, Tara Walmpert Levy, Chris Lien, Adam Lovallo, George Michie, Mike Mothner, Daniel Pearson, George Popstefanov, Jesse Pujji, Matt Quirie, Janelle Ramirez, Alan Ringvald, Soso Sazesh, Brook Schaaf, Jonah Stein, Dave Tan, Fred Vallaeys, Wister Walcott, Jay Weintraub, Terry Whalen, Chris Zaharias, and Kelli Zito.

Last but not least, thank you to the team at Scribe Media who helped me put this book together. Did we set the record for the longest time period from idea to publication? Thanks to Bailey Hayes, Nikki Van Noy, Kacy Wren, AJ Hendrickson, and Areil Sutton.

CPSIA information can be obtained
at www.ICGtesting.com
Printed in the USA
FSHW010221230621
82607FS

9 781544 506623